OpenOffice 3.4
Volume III: Base

quantum scientific publishing

OpenOffice 3.4
Volume III: Base

CHRISTOPHER N. CAIN

RILEY W. WALKER

quantum scientific publishing

OpenOffice 3.4
Volume III: Base

ISBN-13: 978-1480224360
ISBN-10: 1480224367

Published by quantum scientific publishing

Pittsburgh, PA | Copyright © 2012

All rights reserved. Permission in writing must be obtained from the publisher before any part of this work may be reproduced or transmitted in any form, including photocopying and recording.

OpenOffice and the OpenOffice logo are trademarks or registered trademarks of The Apache Software Foundation and/or its affiliates.

Cover design by Scott Sheariss

Unit One

- Section 1.1 – Introduction to OpenOffice Base   2
- Section 1.2 – Using the Different Views in Base   4
- Section 1.3 – Creating a Blank Database   6
- Section 1.4 – Using the Wizard to Create a Table   9
- Section 1.5 – Creating Tables   15
- Section 1.6 – Creating a View in Base   18
- Section 1.7 – Opening an Existing Database   22
- Section 1.8 – Saving a Database in Base   24
- Section 1.9 – Setting the Primary Key   27
- Section 1.10 – Tips and Help Dialog Box   29
- Section 1.11 – Manipulating Table Columns and Rows   33
- Section 1.12 – How to Hide/Unhide Columns   35
- Section 1.13 – Manually Setting the Column Width   38
- Section 1.14 – Importing Data into Base   41
- Section 1.15 – Exporting Database Data   46

Unit Two

- Section 2.1 – Common Database Terms   52
- Section 2.2 – Using Edit, Delete, and Rename From the Toolbar   54
- Section 2.3 – Creating a Form Using a Wizard   59
- Section 2.4 – Using a Switchboard   65
- Section 2.5 – Refining Form Properties   72
- Section 2.6 – Modifying Fields in a Form   76
- Section 2.7 – Using the Custom Color Menu   80
- Section 2.8 – Refining a Form   84
- Section 2.9 – Creating a Split Form   86
- Section 2.10 – Adding Controls to Forms   89
- Section 2.11 – Adding Controls Using the Control Wizard   93
- Section 2.12 – Modifying the Layout of Fields on a Form   98
- Section 2.13 – Creating a Relationship Between Tables   102
- Section 2.14 – Adding a Subform Using a Wizard   105
- Section 2.15 – Adding Symbols and Special Characters   111

Unit Three

Section 3.1 – Sorting Information   116

Section 3.2 – Using the AutoFilter   119

Section 3.3 – Creating a Custom Filter   121

Section 3.4 – Moving Data Using Copy and Cut   124

Section 3.5 – Creating a Query in Design View   127

Section 3.6 – Creating a Query Using the Wizard   131

Section 3.7 – Using the Function Field   136

Section 3.8 – Restricting Data Using Field Type Settings   141

Section 3.9 – Restricting Data Using Field Length Settings   144

Section 3.10 – Creating a Report   146

Section 3.11 – Creating a Report Using the Report Wizard   149

Section 3.12 – Changing the Font, Size, and Color of the Text   156

Section 3.13 – Restricting Data Using the Combo Box   160

Section 3.14 – Updating Information in a Table   165

Section 3.15 – Deleting Information from a Table   167

Appendix

OpenOffice Volume III: Base Answer Key   172

Unit One

Section 1.1 – Introduction to OpenOffice Base 2

Section 1.2 – Using the Different Views in Base 4

Section 1.3 – Creating a Blank Database 6

Section 1.4 – Using the Wizard to Create a Table 9

Section 1.5 – Creating Tables 15

Section 1.6 – Creating a View in Base 18

Section 1.7 – Opening an Existing Database 22

Section 1.8 – Saving a Database in Base 24

Section 1.9 – Setting the Primary Key 27

Section 1.10 – Tips and Help Dialog Box 29

Section 1.11 – Manipulating Table Columns and Rows 33

Section 1.12 – How to Hide/Unhide Columns 35

Section 1.13 – Manually Setting the Column Width 38

Section 1.14 – Importing Data into Base 41

Section 1.15 – Exporting Database Data 46

Section 1.1 – Introduction to OpenOffice Base

Section Objective:

- Learn about OpenOffice Base and what it can be used for.

Introduction

Welcome to OpenOffice Base. Base is a simple yet powerful database tool, and is just one of six applications found within the Apache OpenOffice Suite 3.4. If not already installed, download the lastest version of the Apache OpenOffice Suite from the www.openoffice.org website. When the page loads, click "I want to download OpenOffice" to be directed to the download page. Follow the instructions to complete the download.

This book begins by introducing the basic features and layout of Base, and then progresses to more complex functions and operations. At the end of each section, there are questions which test readers' understanding of the application. Use these questions, as well as the steps provided in this book, to learn many different tasks which can be accomplished in OpenOffice Base.

Features in OpenOffice Base

OpenOffice Base is a tool for managing databases. Databases are structured catalogs of information. In Base, every database is stored in a single file. Databases can store many types of information, including numbers, pages of text, and pictures. Databases can store a lot of information. Everything from simple lists to inventory catalogs can be created in a database. Each database file contains database objects, which are the components of a database. There are six different types of database objects:

- **Tables** – Tables store information. Tables are the main component of any database, and allow users to create as many tables as necessary.

- **Queries** – Queries allow users to quickly perform an action on a table. Most times, this action will involve retrieving certain amounts of information in the table. Users can also set up queries to make changes.

- **Forms** – Forms allow users to create, arrange, and colorize. Forms provide an easy way to view or change the information in a table.

- **Reports** – Reports help users print information in a table. Users have the ability to choose where the information appears on the printed page, how it is grouped and sorted, and how it is formatted.

- **Macros** – Macros are mini-programs that automate custom tasks. Macros are a simple way to get custom results without becoming a programmer.

- **Modules** – Modules are files that contain Visual Basic code. The user can use this code to perform multiple tasks in Base.

Base and Calc perform many of the same tasks when it comes to dealing with lists and tables of information. The reason that it is necessary to learn how to use Base is that while Calc is good for small, simple amounts of information, it cannot handle the same quantity and complexity of information as Base. Base also allows users to maintain multiple lists with related information, while Calc does not.

Another difference between Calc and Base is the complexity of the application's features. Base provides features that allow users to create customized search routines, design fine-tuned forms for data entry, and print a variety of reports.

Growth & Assessment

1. How many types of database objects are there?

2. The application's features differ between Calc and Base.

    a. TRUE

    b. FALSE

3. What are Modules?

4. How are Forms used?

Section 1.2 – Using the Different Views in Base

Section Objective:

- Learn the different views available in OpenOffice Base.

Different Views in OpenOffice Base

OpenOffice Base provides users with two basic views, the **Design view** and the **Data view**. This section will describe both of these basic view options and the necessary steps to switch between them when working in Base.

Data View – Data view shows the data in the database. It also allows users to enter and edit data within the **Tables** and **Forms**. Other than a few minor formatting options, this view does not allow users to modify the format of the database. To access the **Data View**, double-click an existing **Table** or **Form** and Base will adjust the view automatically.

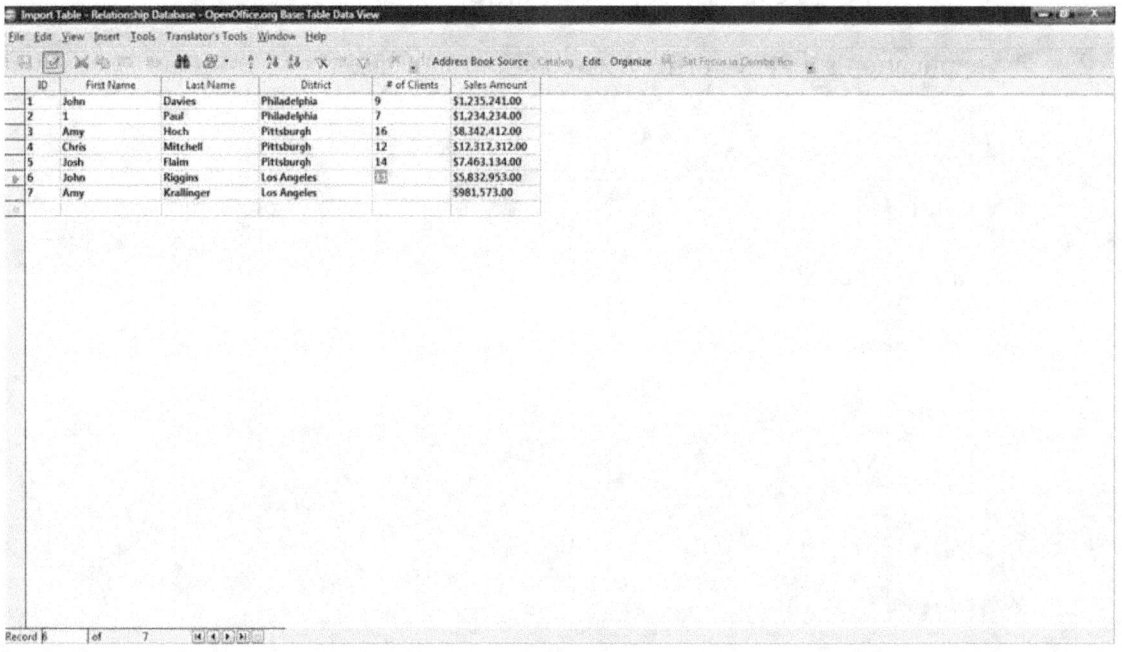

Figure 1

Note – Click the **Edit Data** button on the **Toolbar** to select whether the data can, or cannot, be modified in the Data view.

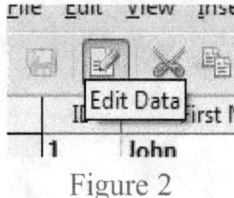

Figure 2

Design View – Design view allows users to create or modify a table, form, or another database object, as well as configure the fields. One limitation of this view is that users are not allowed to change the data within the database. To access the **Design View**, double-click on **Create Form/Table in Design View…**, located in the Table or Form section of the main Base window.

Figure 3

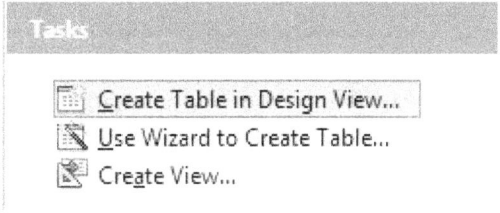

Figure 4

Note – These views are not meant to be used exclusively; meaning, users should switch between these two views while designing and working with the database.

Growth & Assessment

1. Data view shows data in the database.

    a. TRUE

    b. FALSE

2. What are the two basic views in Base?

3. What is the purpose of the Design view?

Section 1.3 – Creating a Blank Database

Section Objective:

- Learn how to create a blank database.

Creating a Blank Database

Before learning how to format and manipulate the different features in OpenOffice Base, users must first learn how to create a blank database. The steps below outline how this is done.

Step 1: Open the Base application by going to the **Start Menu** → **OpenOffice.org** → **OpenOffice Base**. The **Database Wizard** dialog box will appear on the screen.

Figure 1

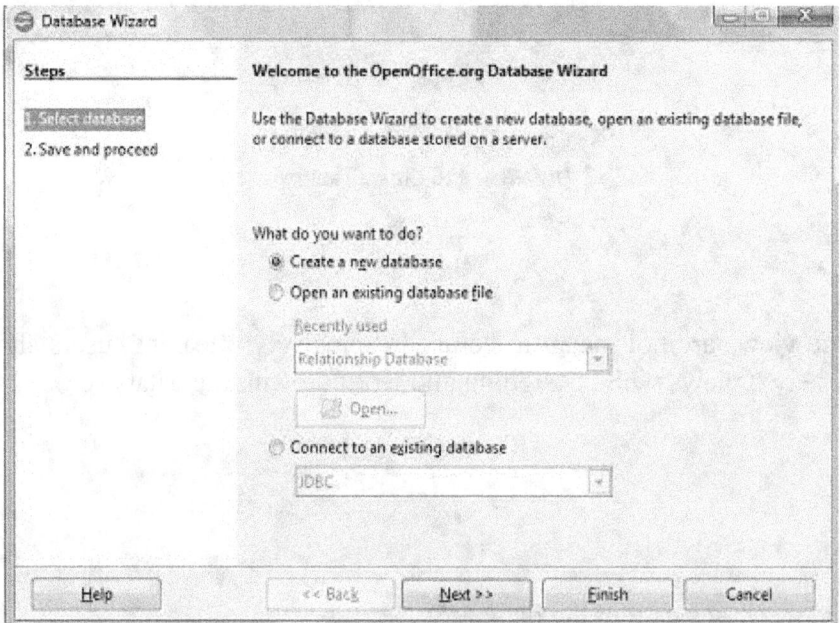

Figure 2

Step 2: Under the **What do you want to do?** portion of the dialog box, the radio button next to **Create a new Database** will already be selected by default.

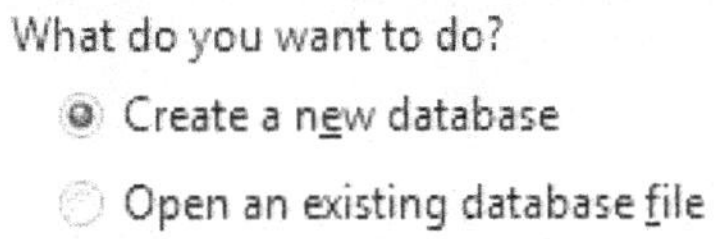

What do you want to do?
- ◉ Create a new database
- ○ Open an existing database file

Figure 3

Step 3: Click the **Next** button. The next step of the wizard allows users to choose whether or not the database is registered. Registering the database tells the main OpenOffice.org application how to handle the different database pages.

Note – Users should register every database created.

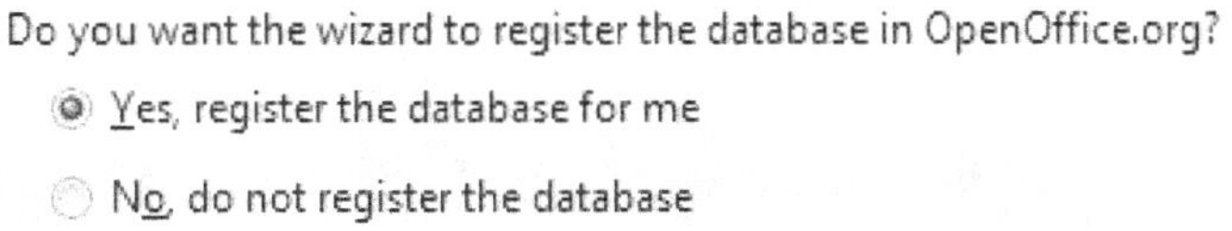

Do you want the wizard to register the database in OpenOffice.org?
- ◉ Yes, register the database for me
- ○ No, do not register the database

Figure 4

Step 4: The next step of the wizard allows users to choose whether the new database should open for manual editing (default selection), or if the new database should open by creating tables using a wizard. For the purpose of this section, leave the default option selected.

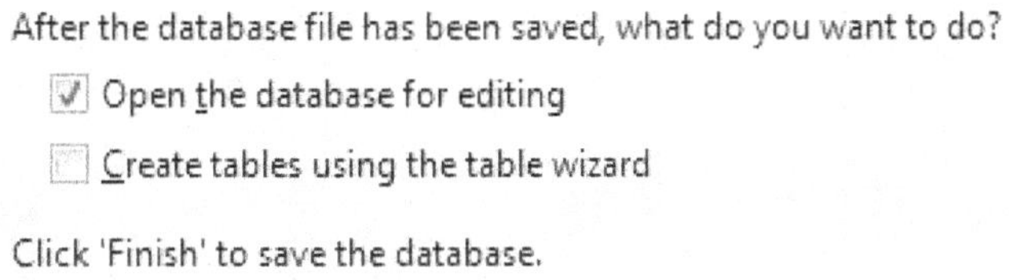

After the database file has been saved, what do you want to do?
- ☑ Open the database for editing
- ☐ Create tables using the table wizard

Click 'Finish' to save the database.

Figure 5

Step 5: Click **Finish**. The **Save As** dialog box will appear.

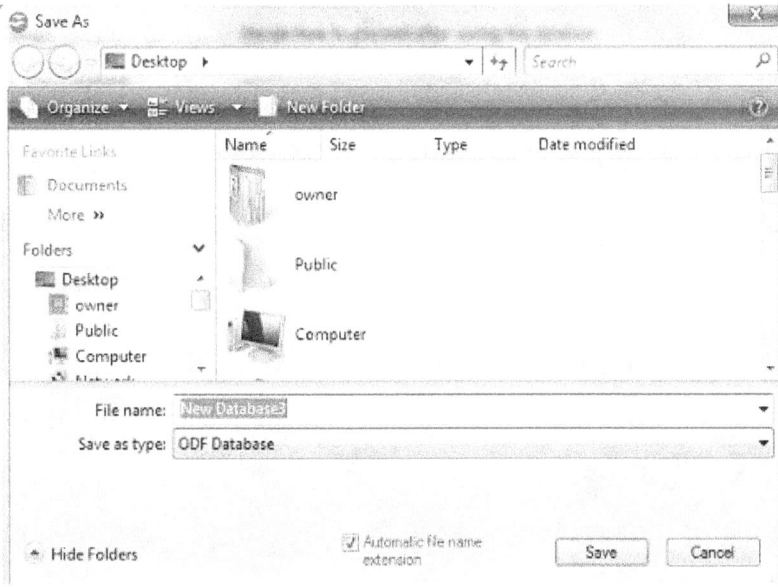

Figure 6

Step 6: In the **File Name** textbox, enter the file name and save it in the preferred folder.

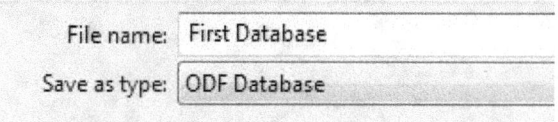

Figure 7

Step 7: Click **Save**. The new blank OpenOffice Base database will open in the application window.

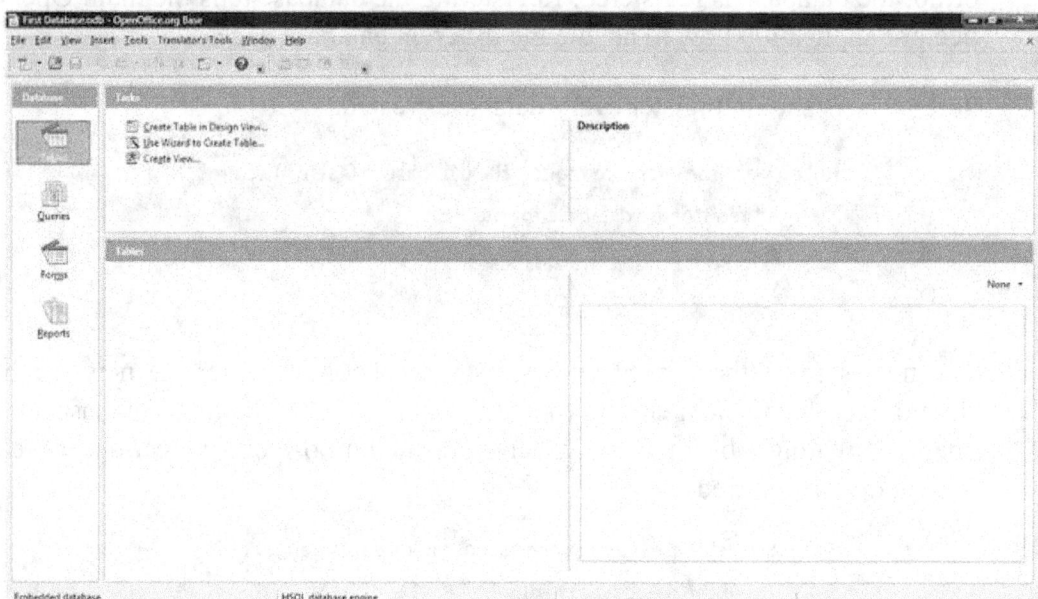

Figure 8

Growth & Assessment

1. Users should register every database created.

    a. TRUE

    b. FALSE

2. What dialog box appears after selecting OpenOffice Base?

3. After registering, what two options are users given?

4. What appears after clicking Finish?

Section 1.4 – Using the Wizard to Create a Table

Section Objective:

- Learn how to create a table using the wizard.

Create a Table Using the Wizard

To start working with OpenOffice Base, users needs to enter data into the database. The process of entering data is done through the use of tables, which act as containers for the data. Users will set up each table with a set of fields that describe the data being inserted. Table fields can be things such as First Name, Address, Invoice Number, etc.

When creating tables in OpenOffice Base, users are provided with a few different options; however, the easiest way is by using the Table Wizard. The Table Wizard provides step by step instructions that help users design a professional looking table with minimal effort. The following steps outline how to use the Table Wizard to create a table in OpenOffice Base.

Step 1: Create a new Base database and navigate to the main Base window.

Figure 1

Step 2: Click the **Tables** icon found in the Database pane on the left-hand side of the Base window.

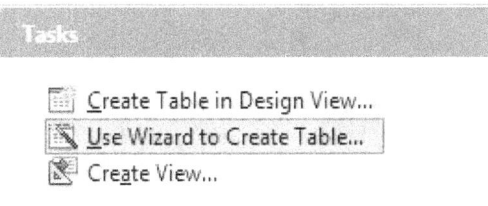

Figure 2

9

Step 3: Double-click on the **Use Wizard to Create Table...** option in the **Tasks** pane at the top of the Base window. The **Table Wizard** dialog box will appear.

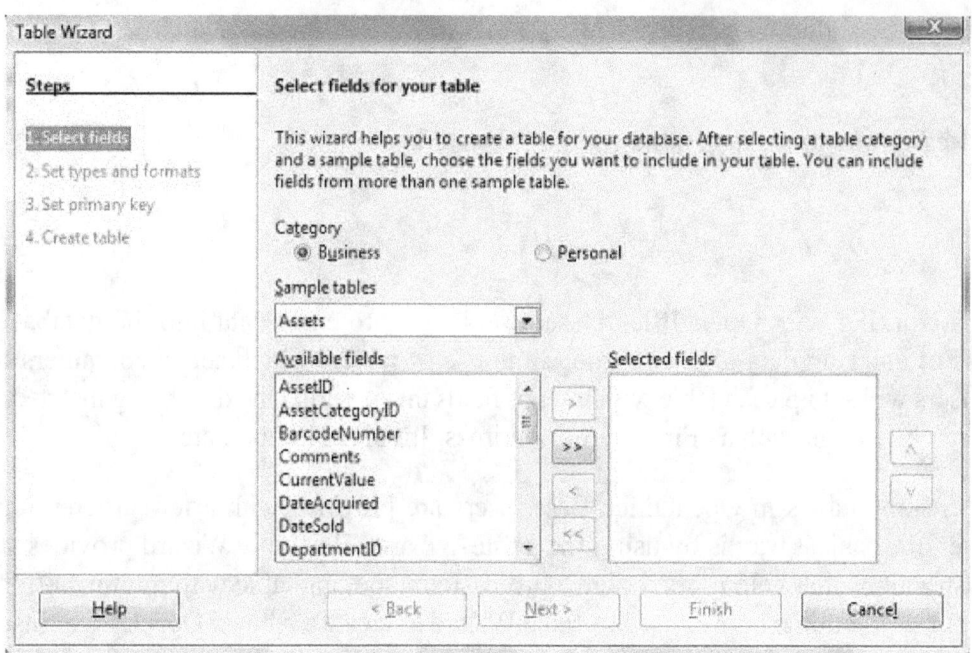

Figure 3

Figure 4

Step 4: The first page of the Table Wizard (the **Select Fields** page), is where users select the types of fields that will be added to the new table. The first option on the Select Fields page is whether the table will be for **business** or for **personal** use. Depending on which radio button is selected, the fields available will differ.

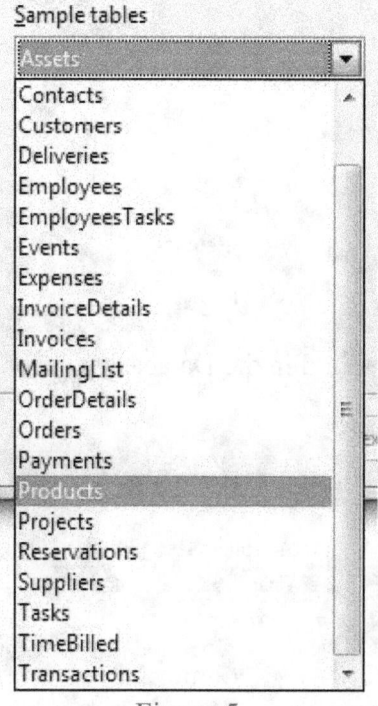

Figure 5

Step 5: The second option on the **Select Fields** page is to select the type of table needed. This is done by reading through the **Sample tables** drop-down. Each sample table contains certain fields based on the intended use of the particular table; however, fields can be added, modified, or deleted in any table selected.

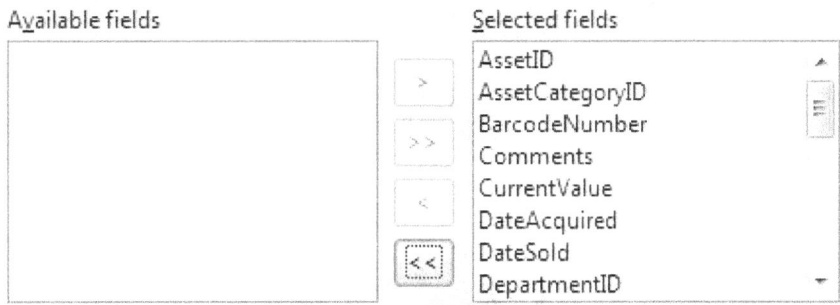

Figure 6

Step 6: The final decision on the **Select Fields** page is to select the fields that will be on the table. The user can click the >> button, to move all of the fields within the **Available fields** window to the **Selected fields** window, or the user can click the > button to move fields individually. Once the desired fields have been moved to the **Selected fields** window, click the **Next** button.

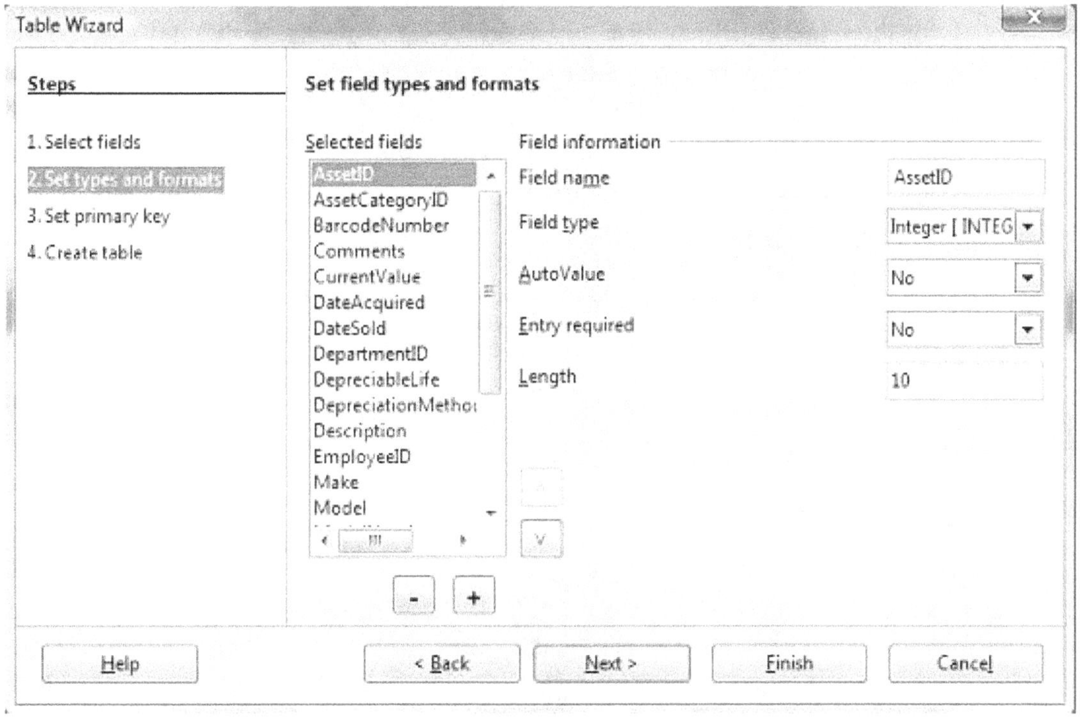

Figure 7

Step 7: The **Set Types and Formats** page of the Table Wizard is where users can customize the selected fields from the previous wizard page. Users have the ability to change things such as the field name, the type of data that can be entered (text, numbers, dates, etc…), and whether the data entry into the field is required. Once the fields have been customized for the intended use, click the **Next** button.

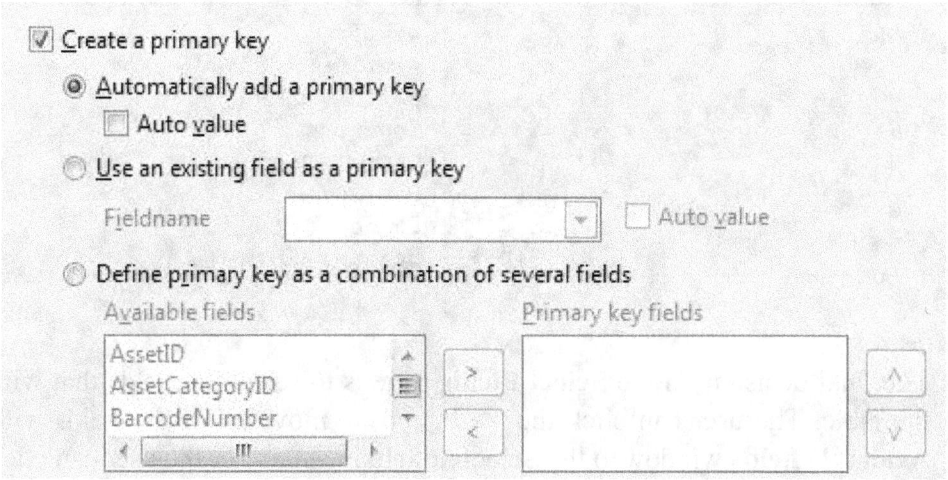

Figure 8

Step 8: The **Set Primary Key** page of the Table Wizard is where users creates a Primary Key for the table. A primary key is a field, or set of fields, with a unique value for each record stored in the table. An example of a field that would be a good primary key, would be an EmployeeID field. Since each employee would have a unique Employee ID, it would fit the Primary Key's criteria of being a unique identifier. Check on the checkbox next to **Create a Primary Key** to activate the other options on the page.

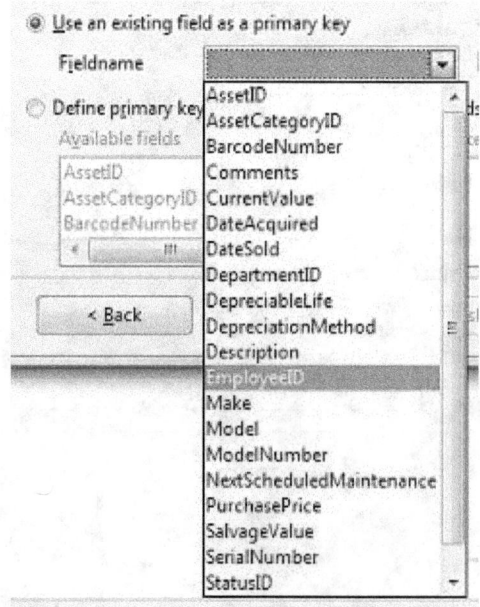

Figure 9

Step 9: Next, the user needs to select which way the primary key will be created. The user is presented with 3 options:

- **Automatically Add a Primary Key** – If this option is chosen, Base will add another field to the data named ID. Clicking the **Auto value** checkbox would cause Base to automatically insert a unique number into the field as the table is populated.

- **Use an Existing Field as a Primary Key** – If this option is chosen, the user can use the drop-down menu to select one of the existing fields to be the primary key.

- **Define Primary Key as a Combination of Several Fields** – This option is very similar to the previous option; however, with this option the user will select multiple fields that come together to form the primary key. An example of this would be First Name and Address. These two fields individually would not make a good primary key, but together they create a unique identifier.

Once a preferred option has been selected, click the **Next** button to continue to the next page of the Table Wizard.

What do you want to name your table?
Wizard Table

Figure 10

Step 10: The final page of the wizard is the **Create Table** page. Here, users has the ability to name the new table and decide how they would like to proceed once the Table Wizard has finished. Enter the table name into the textbox and select one of the three radio buttons (located at the bottom of the wizard), to identify the preferred action after closing the Table Wizard.

What do you want to do next?
◉ Insert data immediately
○ Modify the table design
○ Create a form based on this table

Figure 11

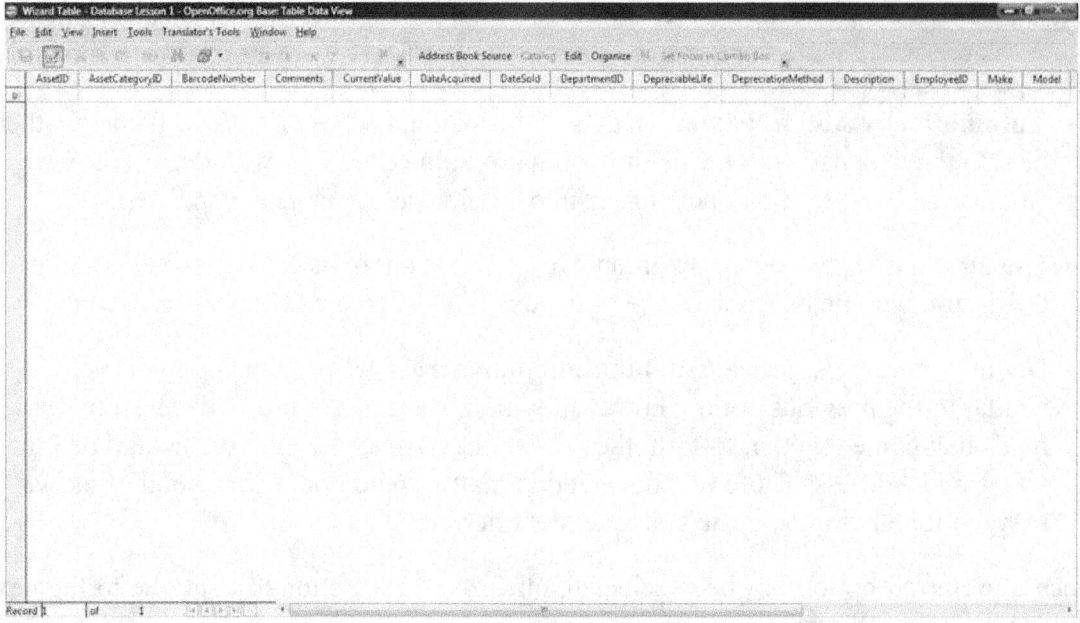

Figure 12

Step 11: Click the **Finish** button. A blank table will be created containing the fields selected in the Table Wizard. Data can now be inserted into the database.

Growth & Assessment

1. What are the three Primary Key options?

2. What is a Primary Key?

3. What is the first page of the Table Wizard used for?

Section 1.5 – Creating Tables

Section Objective:

- Learn how to create tables.

Creating Tables

In OpenOffice Base, databases are made up of one or more tables that contain the needed information in an organized format. A database will usually contain more than one table, and each table will have a fixed number of fields.

This section will provide users with the necessary steps to create a table in Design view. In Design view, users must first create the table's structure and then switch to Data view to enter data into the table. Data can also be entered by some other method, such as pasting or importing data from an outside source. As stated above, each table has a fixed number of fields; each of those fields is comprised of three parts, the **Field Name**, **Field Type**, and **Description**. The following steps describe these three field components and outline the necessary steps for creating a table and inserting data.

Step 1: Create a new Base database.

Step 2: Double-click on the **Create Table in Design View…** link, located in the Task pane. The **Table Design** dialog box will open.

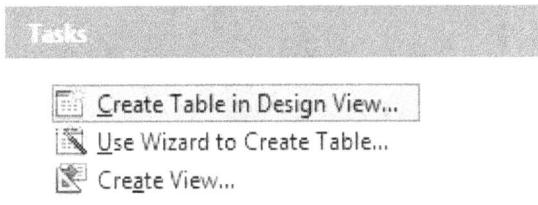

Figure 1

Step 3: In the **Field Name** column, type the preferred field name and then press the **Tab** button. The **Field Type** will be highlighted.

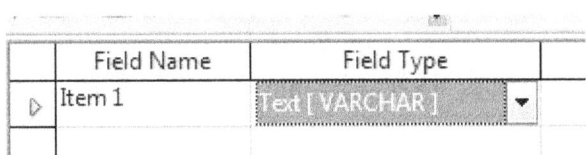

Figure 2

Step 4: In the **Field Type** column, click on the pull-down menu to see the different field types available. Once the preferred Field Type has been selected, press the **Tab** button to move to the **Description** column.

Note – By Default, the Field Type is set to **Text [VARCHAR]**.

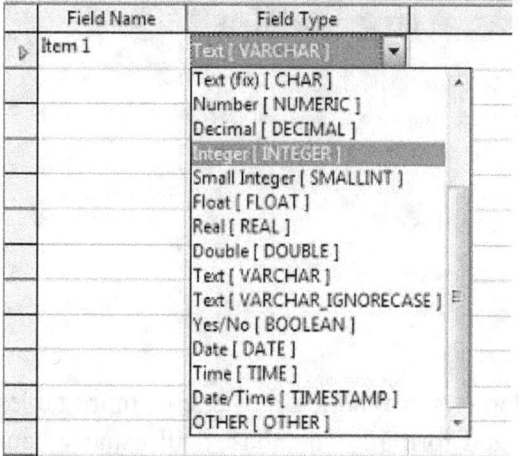

Figure 3

Step 5: Within the **Description** column, users have the ability to type any information that will clarify what type of data should be inserted into each field. Once the desired text has been entered into the Description column, repeat **Steps 3** through **Step 5** for every additional field inserted into the table.

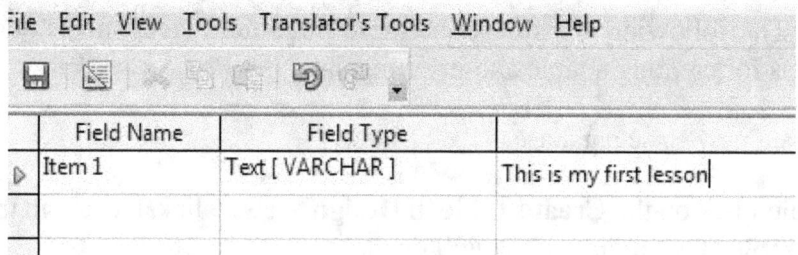

Figure 4

Step 6: Once all desired fields have been entered into the table, click the **Save** button located on the Menu Bar.

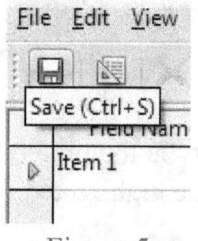

Figure 5

Step 7: Enter the preferred table name and click the **OK** button.

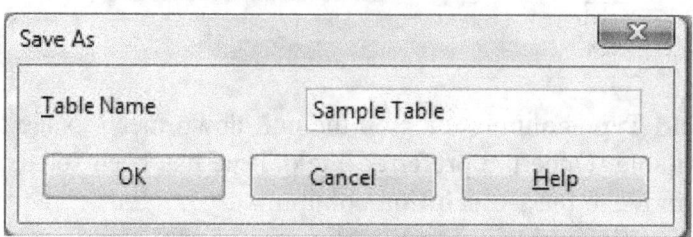

Figure 6

Step 8: Close the **Table Design** dialog box to return to the application's main window. The table has now been created and can be accessed at any time.

Figure 7

Growth & Assessment

1. In Design view, users must first create the table's structure.

    a. TRUE

    b. FALSE

2. What is the purpose of the Description column?

3. By default, what is the Field Type column set to?

4. How many field parts are there?

Section 1.6 – Creating a View in Base

Section Objective:

- Learn how to create a view.

Creating a View

OpenOffice Base provides the user with the ability to create a view as a way of looking at a table differently. A view is a specific subset of data within a table; showing all or some of the fields, and all or some of the records. This section will outline how a user can use a view to restrict the data fields that are displayed when looking at table data.

Before following the steps below, create a table labeled "**Customer**" that contains the following data.

Customer Number	First Name	Last Name	City	State
1	Amy	Mitchell	Pittsburgh	PA
2	Bob	Salzer	Philadelphia	PA
3	Ryan	Dunn	Chester	PA
4	John	Davies	Bedford	PA

Figure 1

Step 1: Click the **Tables** icon located in the **Database** pane on the left-hand side of the Base window.

Figure 2

Step 2: In the **Tasks** pane, located at the top of the Base window, double-click **Create View…**. The **View Design** window will appear with the **Add Tables** dialog box displayed.

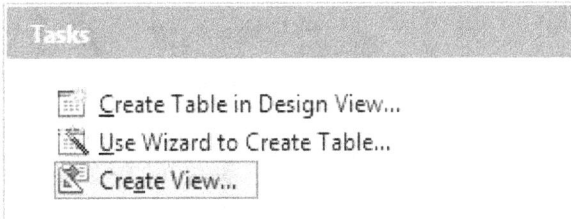

Figure 3

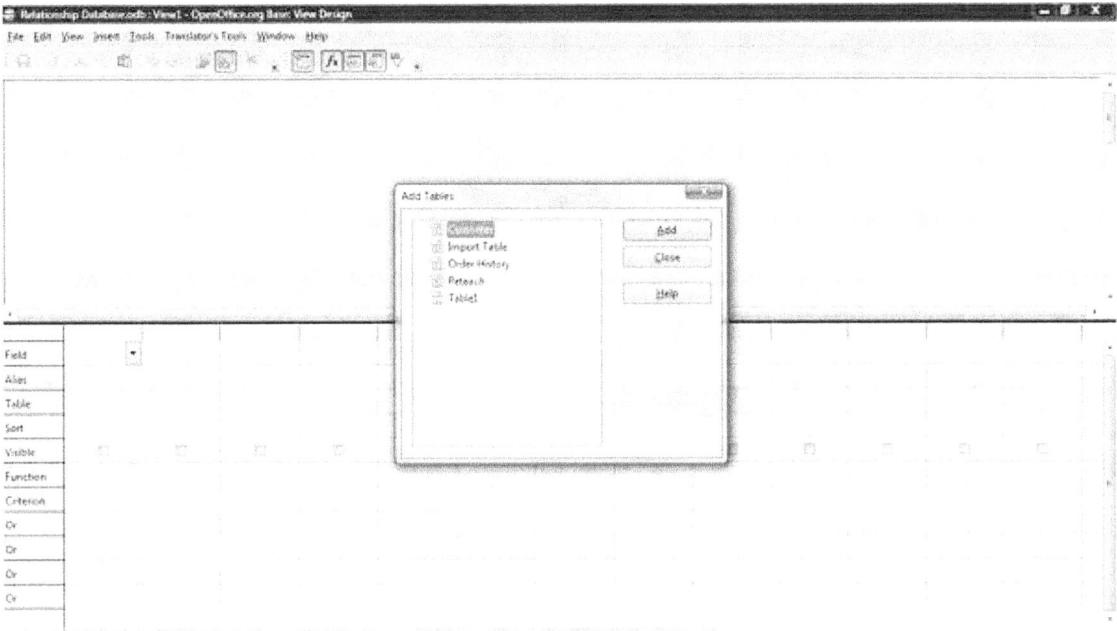

Figure 4

Step 3: Select the desired "**Customer**" table and click **Add**. The table will be displayed in the **View Design** window.

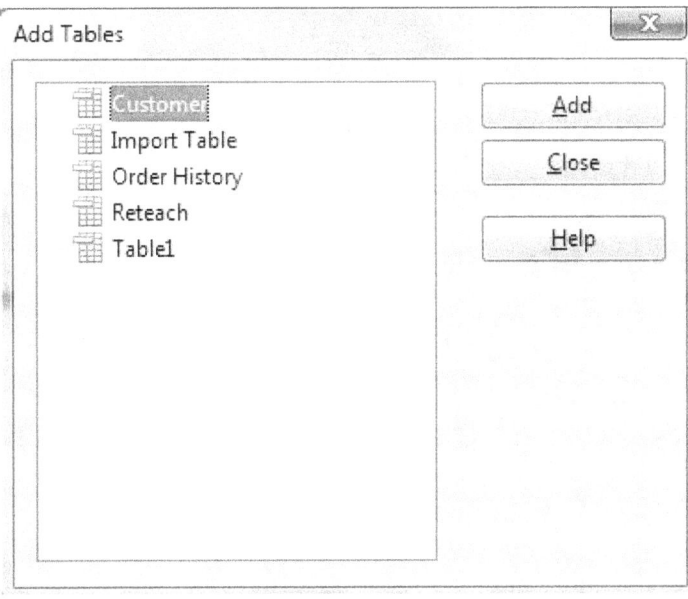

Figure 5

Step 4: Click **Close** to finish adding tables, and to close the **Add Tables** window.

Step 5: Double-click the **First Name** field and the **Last Name** field located in the small floating window on the **View Design** page. This will cause the two fields to be placed in the chart at the bottom of the page.

Field	First Name	Last Name	
Alias			
Table	Customer	Customer	
Sort			
Visible	✓	✓	☐
Function			

Figure 6

Step 6: Once the desired fields have been selected, save the view by opening the **File** menu and selecting **Save**.

Note – Clicking the diskette icon in the top left-hand corner of the toolbar will also save the view.

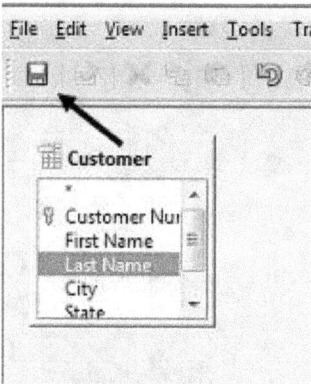

Figure 7

Step 7: The **Save As** dialog box will appear. Enter the preferred name for the recently created view, and click **Save**.

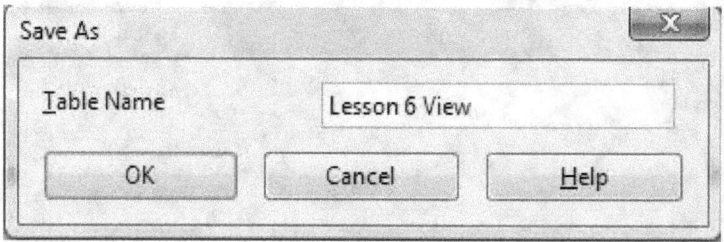

Figure 8

20

Step 8: After saving, close the **View Design** window.

> **Note** – The created view will be listed with the Tables. To display the view, double-click on the view name and it will open.

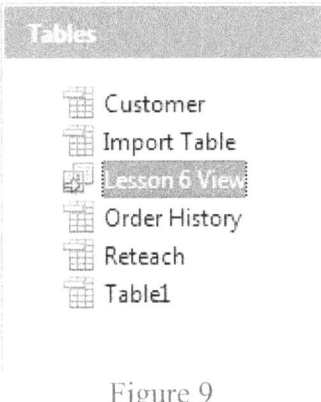

Figure 9

Growth & Assessment

1. OpenOffice Base provides users with the ability to create a view as a way of looking at a table differently.

    a. TRUE

    b. FALSE

2. Besides selecting Save, what is the other saving method?

3. Where is the Tables icon located?

Section 1.7 – Opening an Existing Database

Section Objective:

- Learn how to open an existing database.

Opening an Existing Database

In OpenOffice Base, there are three common ways of opening an existing database. These options are described below:

Clicking the File Icon

The first way a user is able to open a database is by locating the existing database on the computer, right-click the file name and select **Open**.

Note – Double-clicking the file name will also open the existing database.

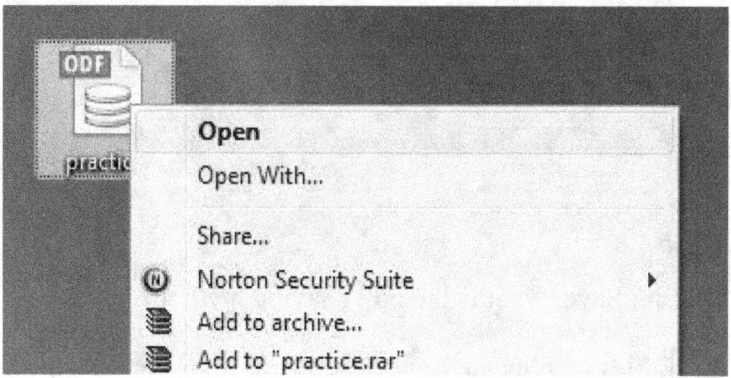

Figure 1

Clicking the Radio Button

The second way a user is able to open a database is by clicking the radio button next to **Open an existing database file**. The Database Wizard window will appear and the user can search and select the desired database file from the displayed listing.

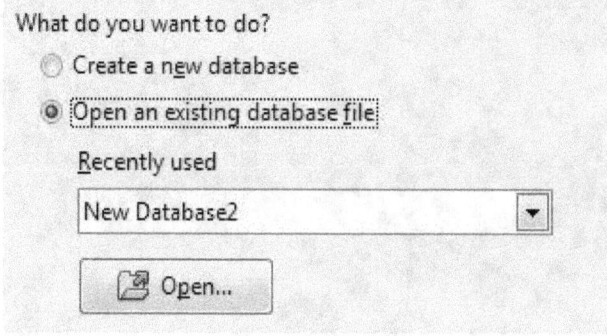

Figure 2

Going Through the File Menu

The third and final way a user is able to open a database is by going through the File menu. From the File menu, select **Open** and the Open dialog box will appear. Using the Open dialog box, browse for the desired OpenOffice.org database file.

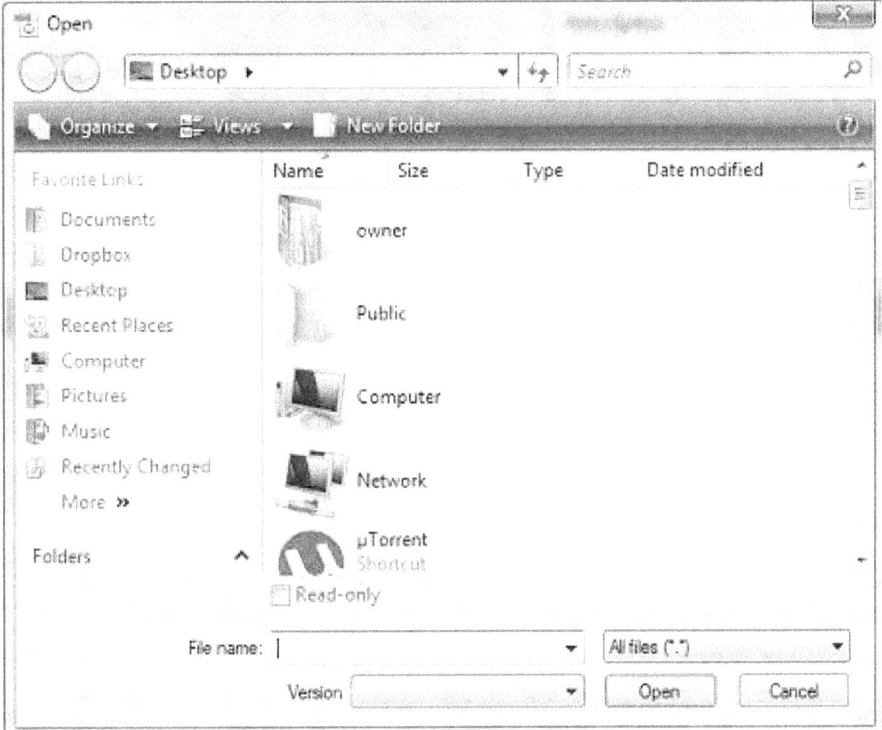

Figure 3

Growth & Assessment

1. How many ways can an existing database be opened?

2. Double-clicking a Base file will open it.

    a. TRUE

    b. FALSE

3. Using the File menu method, explain the steps to open an existing file.

Section 1.8 – Saving a Database in Base

Section Objective:

- Learning how to save a database in Base.

Saving a Database

In OpenOffice Base, saving a database is different than saving a document in any other application in the OpenOffice Suite. In Base, users are forced to name and save the database before it is created. This is helpful because it allows users to easily save the database using keyboard shortcuts rather than going through the Menu Bar. This is also helpful because it permits users from accidentally deleting any unsaved work. This section will outline how to set up and saves a database, prior to working on it.

Steps for Saving a Database:

Step 1: Create a new blank database. The **Database Wizard** will provide the necessary steps to create the database. Once the last step of the wizard has been reached, click **Finish**. The Database Wizard will close and the **Save As** dialog box will appear.

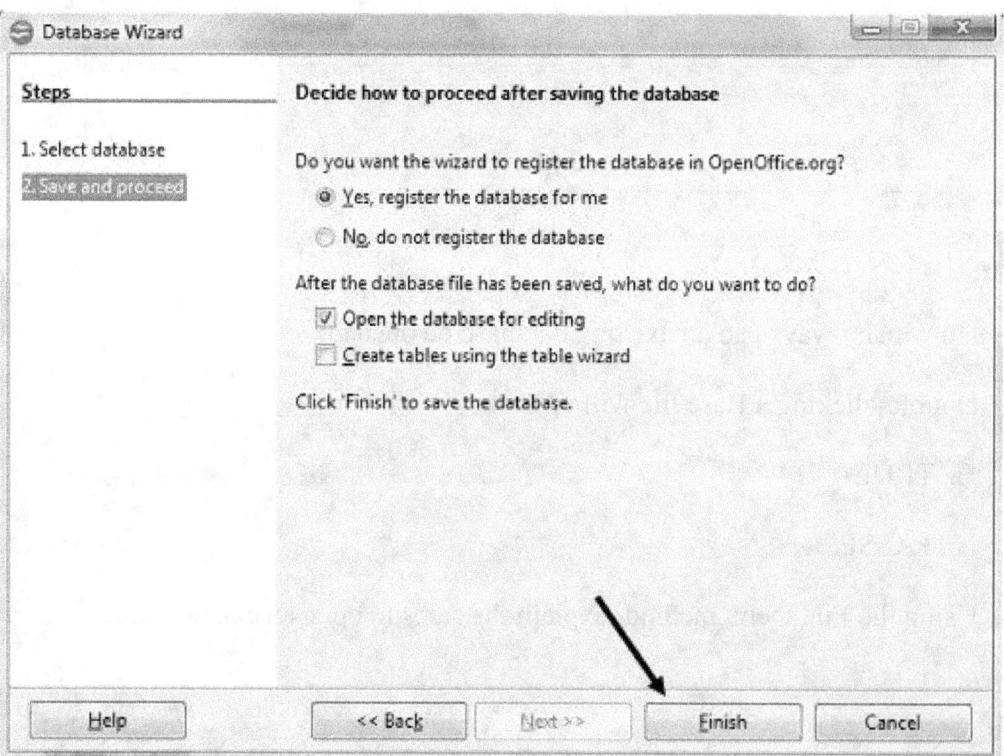

Figure 1

Step 2: Within the Save As dialog box, choose the desired location in which to save the database by selecting a folder in the **Save In** window.

Figure 2

Step 3: In the **File Name** textbox, enter a preferred name.

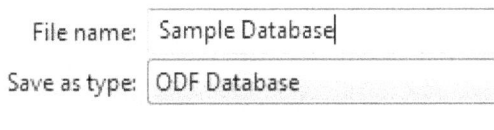

Figure 3

Step 4: Once the database has been named, click **Save**. The name of the database will be visible in the application's title bar.

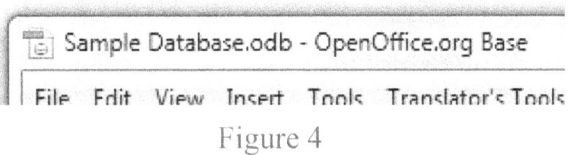

Figure 4

Using the Save Command

Use the Save command when saving a database that has already been saved at least one time. Using the Save command frequently is recommended because it ensures that the project being worked on will not be lost if a computer error occurs. This is done by pressing **CTRL + S** or, from the **File** menu, selecting **Save**.

Note – If a user selects the Save command and has not previously saved the database, the **Save As** dialog box will appear.

Databases are made up of various components, such as Tables, Forms, Queries and Reports. With this many database elements, it is sometimes difficult to know if every element has been saved. Base helps in this regard by providing users with a **Save All** option which can be accessed through the File menu. Once **Save All** has been selected, every element within the database will be saved.

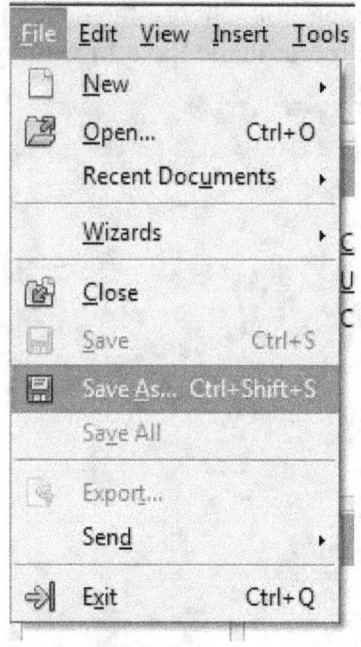

Figure5

Growth & Assessment

1. In Base, saving a database is different than saving a document in any other application in the OpenOffice Suite.

    a. TRUE

    b. FALSE

2. What is the keyboard shortcut for Save?

3. In Base, users will be forced to name and save the database before it is created.

    a. TRUE

    b. FALSE

4. How would a user save all parts of a database at once?

Section 1.9 – Setting the Primary Key

Section Objective:

- Learn how to set the primary key.

Setting the Primary Key

When setting up tables in the Design view of OpenOffice Base, users have the ability to set the Primary key. The **Primary key** is a field that is unique for each record. Every table that is created in Base must have a primary key. Primary keys are important because they prevent users from having duplicate records within a table. For example, if a user is setting up a list of employees for a company, they may use an employee's social security number as the primary key because every employee entered into the database will have a unique social security number. Base will automatically create a primary key for users when a table is created; however, if it is created from the Design View, users must create their own primary key. The following steps outline how this is done.

Step 1: Create a new OpenOffice Base database and start a new table in Design View.

Step 2: Enter the preferred table name into the **Field Name** column.

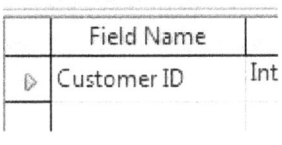

Figure 1

Step 3: Use the arrow to the right of "**Text[VARCHAR]**" under the **Field Type** column to scroll for the needed **Data Type**.

Step 4: Select the needed **Data Type** for the field.

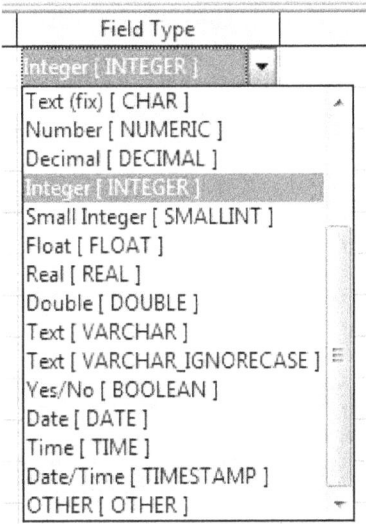

Figure 2

Step 5: Right-click the green arrow, found to the right of the recently created field, and select **Primary Key**.

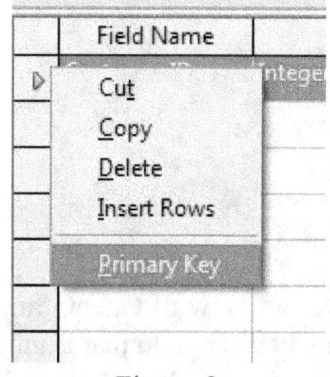

Figure 3

Note – Users have the ability to change the table's primary key field at any time.

Growth & Assessment

1. Why are Primary Keys important?

2. Base will automatically create a primary key when a table is created.

    a. TRUE

    b. FALSE

3. If a table is created from Data view, users must create their own Primary Key.

    a. TRUE

    b. FALSE

4. If a user desires to set up a database of employees, what is the benefit of using social security numbers?

Section 1.10 – Tips and Help Dialog Box

Section Objectives:

- Learn how to get help with OpenOffice Base using Tips.

- Learn how to get help with OpenOffice Base using the Help Dialog Box.

Using Tips in OpenOffice Base

OpenOffice Base provides features meant to help and guide the user when something within the application is unfamiliar. There may be times when working in Base that the user wants to do something but doesn't know how. If this is the case, the application provides several ways for the user to get help. Below, these helpful features of Base are described and the necessary steps for accessing them are provided.

Tips

Tips display when the cursor is positioned over many of the UI elements in OpenOffice Base. Tips contain the names of buttons, as well as other useful information.

What's This?

What's This? is a tool in Base that will show the user extended tips about the buttons available on the application's different toolbars. **What's This?** can also be helpful if the user doesn't know the functionality of a command, or what a particular button is used for.

To use the What's This? feature, open the **Help** menu, select **What's This?**. Then, position the cursor over any button to see an explanation of its functionality and use.

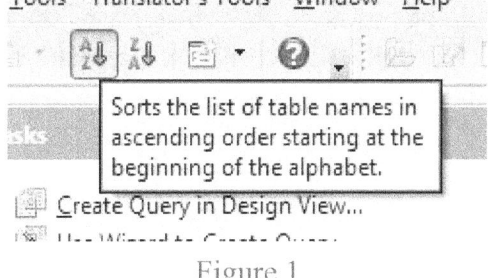

Figure 1

What's This?: Extended Tips

As stated above, **Extended tips** inform the user of a button's functionality and uses. Extended tips will be displayed from the What's This? tool until the user clicks somewhere within the database. The extended tips can also be enabled to always display. This can be done by opening the **Tools** menu, selecting **Options**, clicking **General** (on the left, under OpenOffice.org), and then checking both the "**tips**" and "**extended tips**" checkboxes. By enabling the Extended tips, the user is provided with a description of a button's functionality without having to access the Help menus.

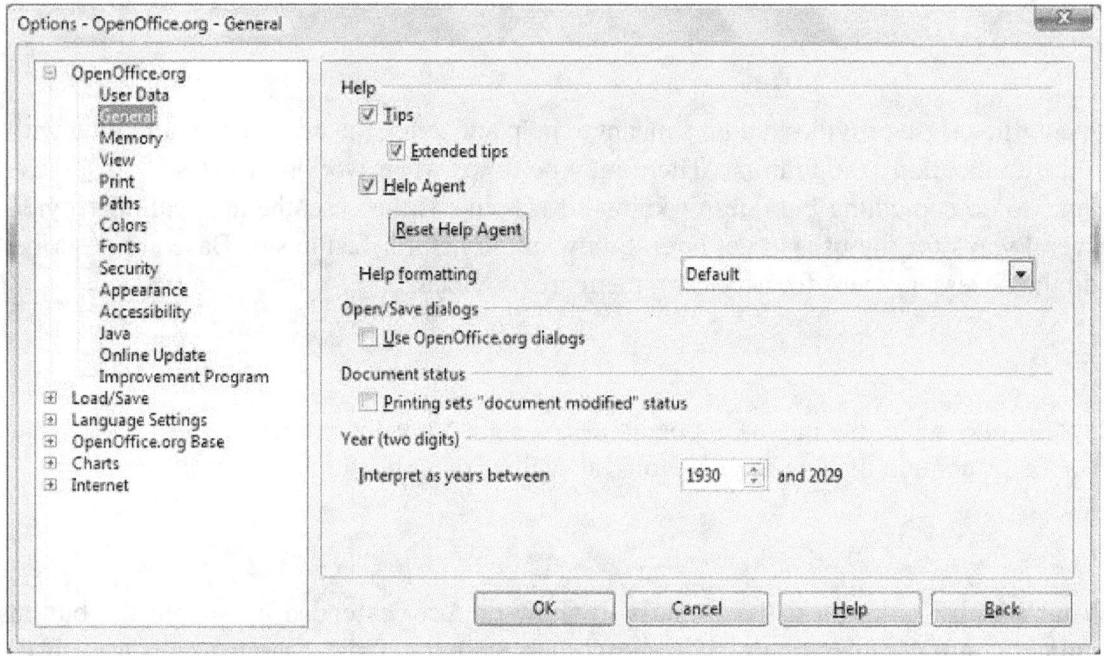

Figure 2

The Help Menu

If a user can't find an answer by using the What's This? feature, they can search for it in the **Help** menu. The **Help** dialog box is accessed by clicking the **Help Button**, which is the small question mark in the top right-hand corner of the **Toolbar**. For further explanation, follow the steps below which outline how a user can find help when trying to create a table in Base.

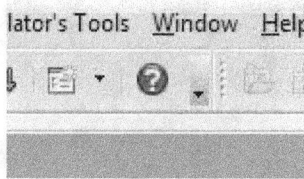

Figure 3

Step 1: Click on the **Find** tab along the top of the **Help** dialog box. In the **Search** textbox, type "**Creating a Table**."

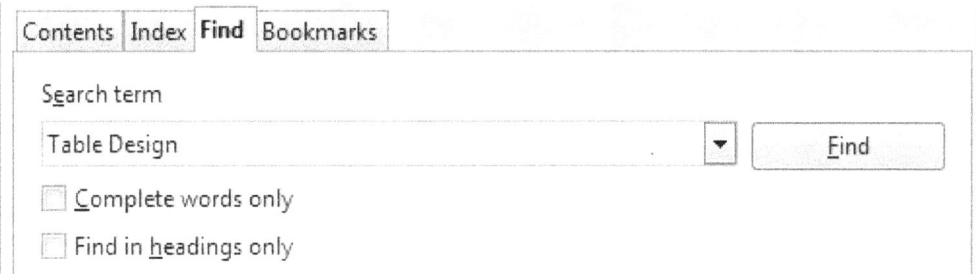

Figure 4

Step 2: Press **Enter** or click **Find**. The search results appear in the Help dialog box.

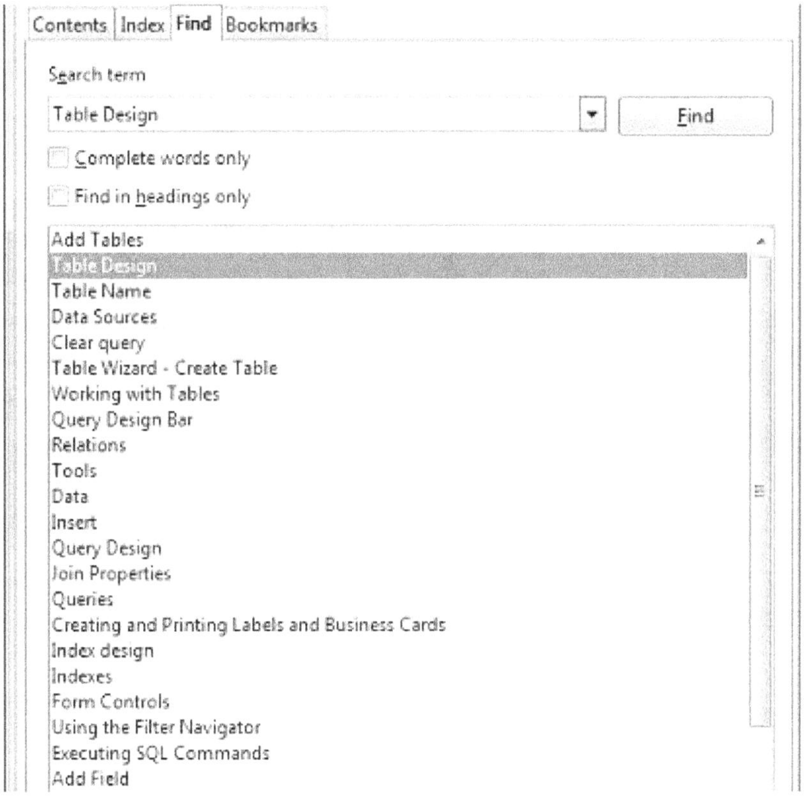

Figure 5

Step 3: From the list of found topics within the Help dialog box, select **Table Design**. A description of how to work with tables in Base will be displayed on the screen.

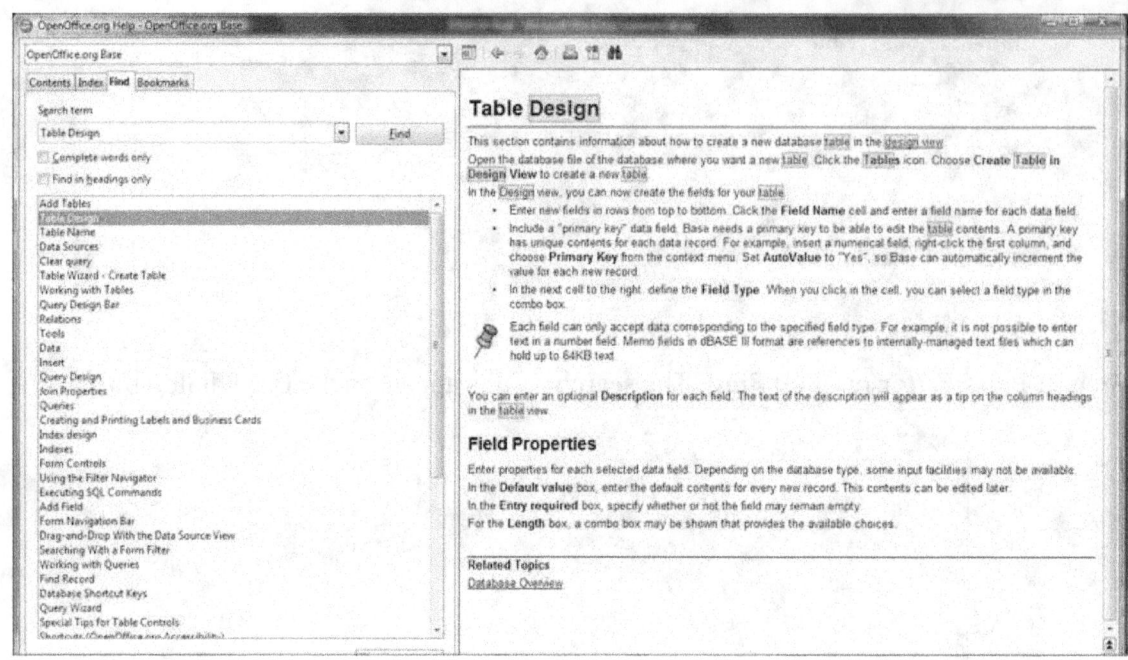

Figure 6

Step 4: Once the needed information has been obtained, close the Help dialog box.

> **Note** – The same information can be found in the **Contents** and **Index** tabs located in the Help dialog box.

Figure 7

Growth & Assessment

1. When will Extended tips no longer be active from the What's This? tool?

2. If a user can't find the answer to a question by using What's This?, the user can search for it in the Help menu.

    a. TRUE

    b. FALSE

3. What is the purpose of the What's This? tool?

Section 1.11 – Manipulating Table Columns and Rows

Section Objective:

- Learning how to manipulate table columns and rows.

Altering a Table's Columns and Rows

Once a table has been created in OpenOffice Base, users have the ability to rearrange and resize the table's column and rows to the preferred width. The fields in a datasheet are laid out from left to right, in the order in which they were created. As the user adds more information into the table, certain columns in the datasheet may become too wide or narrow for the information contained within them. If this is the case, users can alter the width of columns and rows to better fit the entered data. In Base, users can change the widths of columns in the following ways:

- **Resizing a single column** – Move the cursor to the right edge of the desired column. Using the left mouse button, drag left to shrink the column, or drag right to make the column wider.

- **Resizing a column to fit its content** – Double-click the edge of the desired column. Base will adjust the column's width equal to the size needed to fit the information contained within the widest cell of the column.

- **Using the Column Width dialog box** – Right-click the heading of the desired column and select **Column Width**. Enter the preferred column width and click **OK**.

Figure 1

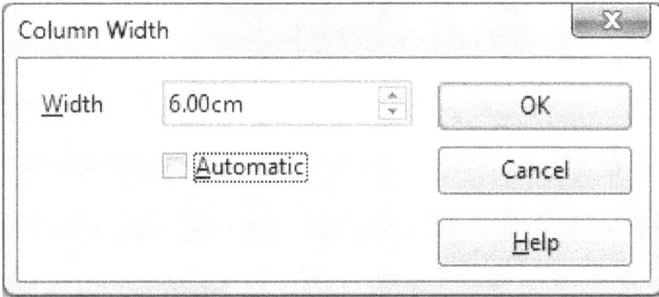

Figure 2

Note – These same techniques can be used to change the Row Height; however, when the row height is changed, it affects all rows within the table.

Growth & Assessment

1. Once a table has been created in OpenOffice Base, the user has the ability to rearrange and resize the table's column and rows to the preferred width.

    a. TRUE

    b. FALSE

2. Explain how to resize a single column.

3. How does a user use the Column Width dialog box?

Section 1.12 – How to Hide/Unhide Columns

Section Objective:

- Learn how to hide/unhide columns and why they would want to do that.

Hide and Unhide Columns

When working in OpenOffice Base, many of the databases created will contain more columns than can be displayed on the screen. This will cause the observer to have to scroll to the left or right to see the columns that are not displayed. In some situations, not all of the columns will need to be displayed at the same time. If this is the case, the user can temporarily hide the unneeded columns. Once hidden, the user can easily display the columns by choosing to unhide them. The following steps outline how to hide and then unhide columns within a database.

Step 1: Open an existing database that has been previously created in Base.

Step 2: Create a new table that has the same headings as the table shown in the figure below. Fill in the empty cells with the desired values.

Customer Number	First Name	Last Name	City	State
1	Amy	Mitchell	Pittsburgh	PA
2	Bob	Salzer	Philadelphia	PA
3	Ryan	Dunn	Chester	PA
4	John	Davies	Bedford	PA

Figure 1

Step 3: Select the **Column Heading** of the **First Name** column. This will highlight the entire column.

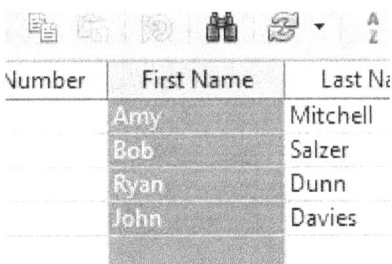

Figure 2

Hide Columns

Step 4: Right-click the selection, and select **Hide Columns**. The selected column will be hidden.

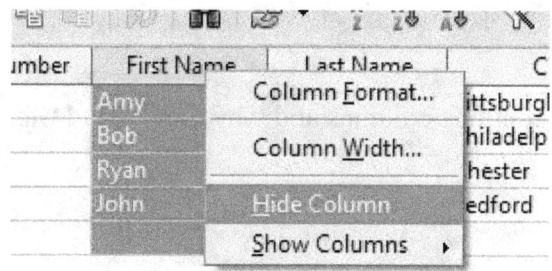

Figure 3

Customer Number	Last Name	City	State
1	Mitchell	Pittsburgh	PA
2	Salzer	Philadelphia	PA
3	Dunn	Chester	PA
4	Davies	Bedford	PA

Figure 4

Show Columns

Step 5: To have the column reappear, right-click any column header and choose **Show Columns**. The column previously hidden will reappear.

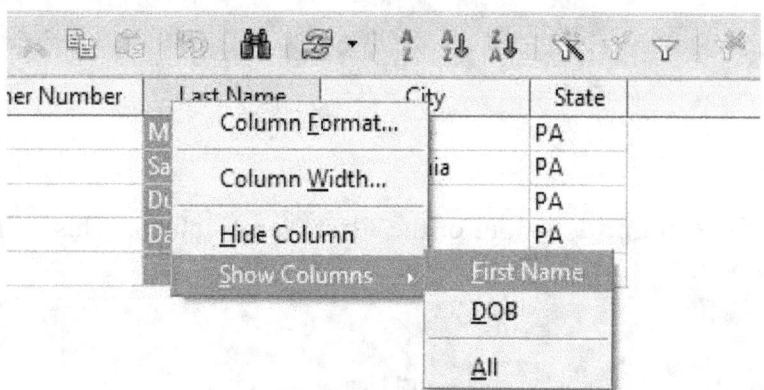

Figure 5

Note – If a user adds a new record while columns are hidden, they will not be able to supply a value for that specific field.

Growth & Assessment

1. Many of the databases created will contain more columns than can be displayed on the screen.

    a. TRUE

    b. FALSE

2. What happens if a user adds a new record while columns are hidden?

3. What does a user have to do in order to make the columns reappear?

4. While working within a database, hiding columns will permanently remove them from the window.

    a. TRUE

    b. FALSE

Section 1.13 – Manually Setting the Column Width

Section Objective:

- Learn how to manually set the column width in a table.

Setting Column Width

In OpenOffice Base, depending on the amount of data inserted into the database table fields, users may want to either expand or contract the size of the columns used in the table. This section explains how to manually expand or contract the size of a column using the mouse, and how to modify columns by using the Quick Menu.

Before following the steps below, create a new table in Base and insert the data shown in the figure below.

Customer Number	First Name	Last Name	City	State
1	Amy	Mitchell	Pittsburgh	PA
2	Bob	Salzer	Philadelphia	PA
3	Ryan	Dunn	Chester	PA
4	John	Davies	Bedford	PA

Figure 1

Changing Cell Width Using the Mouse

Step 1: Click the heading on the **Last Name** field so the entire column is highlighted.

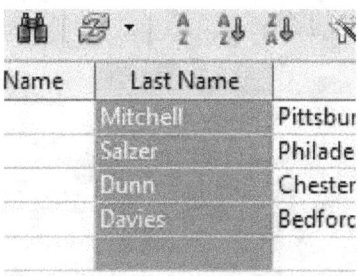

Figure 2

Step 2: Place the cursor on the border between the **Last Name** field name and the **Department** field name so the cursor changes shape.

Step 3: Click and hold the left mouse button and drag the cursor to the right; this will expand the column width. When the column is the desired width, release the left mouse button and the column will remain at the new width.

Figure 3

Changing the Column Width Using the Quick Menu

Step 1: Using the same table, click on the heading for the **First Name** column.

Step 2: Right-click anywhere within the highlighted column to display the **Quick Menu**.

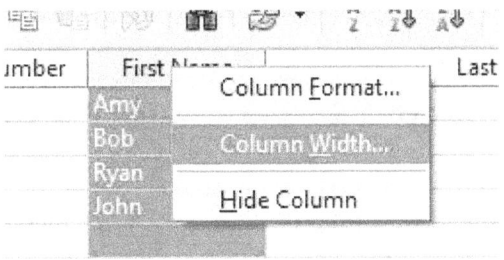

Figure 4

Step 3: Select **Column Width...** from the Quick Menu. The **Column Width** dialog box will appear.

Step 4: Use the arrows to set the column width, or type the desired value into the textbox.

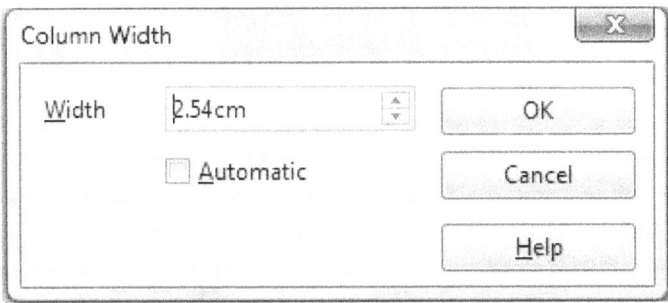

Figure 5

Step 5: Click **Ok**. The Column will be formatted to the new width.

Note – If the checkbox next to **Automatic** in the **Column Width** dialog box is selected, the column cell will automatically format itself to the width of the widest entry.

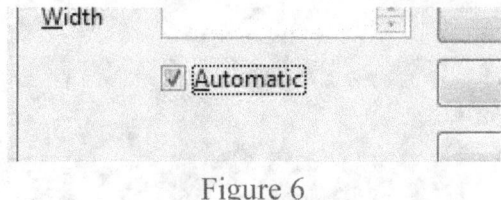

Figure 6

Growth & Assessment

1. The width of columns can be edited?

    a. TRUE

    b. FALSE

2. What happens if the checkbox next to Automatic in the Column Width dialog box is selected?

3. Column width cannot be modified through the Quick Menu.

    a. TRUE

    b. FALSE

Section 1.14 – Importing Data into Base

Section Objective:

- Learn how to import data into OpenOffice Base.

Importing Data

OpenOffice Base allows users to import data from other applications and insert it into a Base database. This is helpful when a user has a large amount of data in an OpenOffice Calc spreadsheet and wishes to analyze the data further using the tools and features of Base. The following steps outline how this is done.

Step 1: Open a Calc spreadsheet with a significant amount of data stored within it.

	A	B	C	D	E
1	First Name	Last Name	District	# of Clients	Sales Amount
2	John	Davies	Philadelphia	9	$1,235,241.00
3	Ken	Paul	Philadelphia	7	$1,234,234.00
4	Amy	Hoch	Pittsburgh	16	$8,342,412.00
5	Chris	Mitchell	Pittsburgh	12	$12,312,312.00
6	Josh	Flaim	Pittsburgh	14	$7,463,134.00
7	John	Riggins	Los Angeles	11	$5,832,953.00
8	Amy	Krallinger	Los Angeles	6	$981,573.00

Figure 1

Step 2: Highlight the desired rows and/or columns that will be imported into the Base database.

Step 3: Once the cells have been highlighted, click the **Data Sources** button on the **Toolbar**.

Figure 2

Note – Directly above the spreadsheet the external data window will open listing all of the databases that have been previously created in Base.

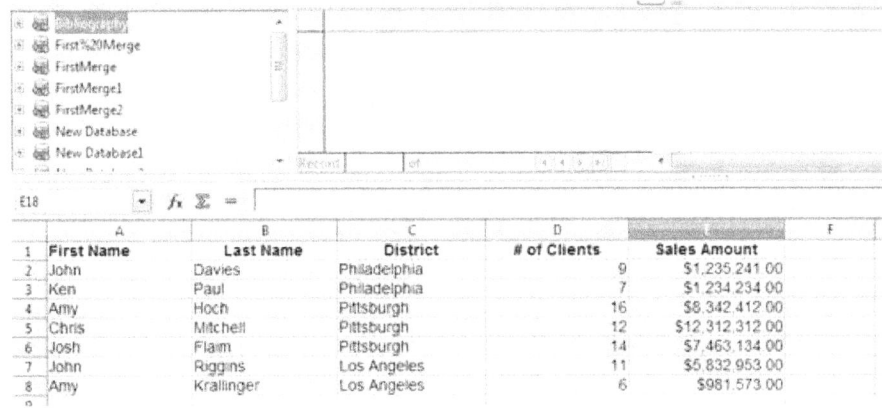

Figure 3

Step 4: Click the plus sign next to any of the existing databases to expand the folders contained within them. In most situations users will see the **Tables** and **Queries** folders.

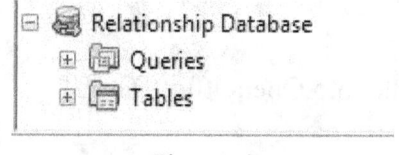

Figure 4

Step 5: Using the left mouse button, click and drag the highlighted data from Calc into the **Tables** folder. Once the cursor is positioned over the Tables folder, release the left mouse button to drop the copied cells into the folder. If the data has been moved from Calc correctly, the **Copy Table** dialog box will appear.

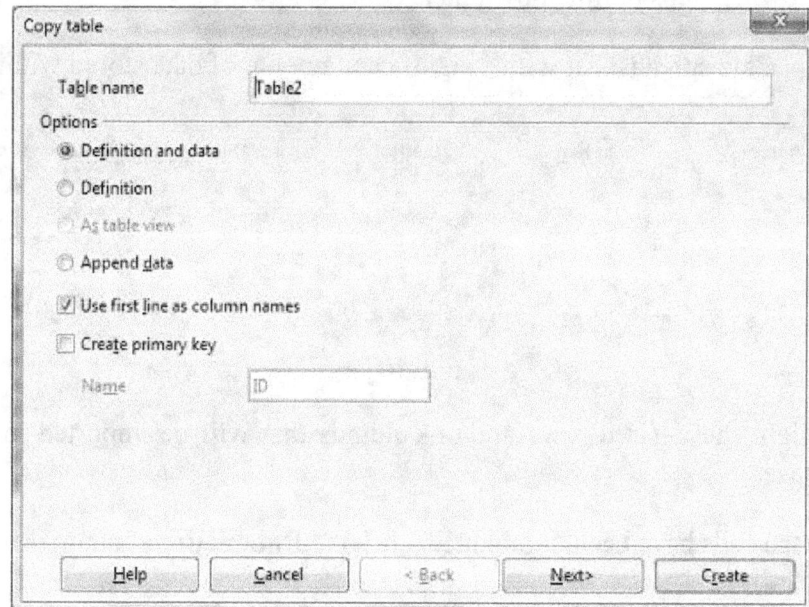

Figure 5

Step 6: In the **Table Name** textbox, enter a name for the new table in which the imported data will be placed.

Figure 6

Step 7: Within the **Options** portion of the dialog box, select **Definition and data**, because a new table is being created.

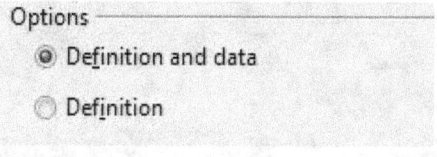

Figure 7

Step 8: If the first row, in the cells selected from Calc, is a heading, select the checkbox next to **Use first line as column names**.

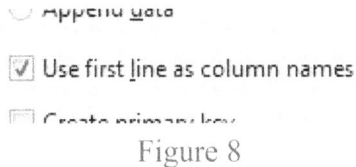

Figure 8

Step 9: The final section of the dialog box allows users to set the **Primary Key** for the imported data. Select the checkbox next to **Create primary key** so the **Name** field becomes active.

Figure 9

Step 10: Enter the preferred name for the Primary Key row. Click **Next** to move to the **Apply columns** textbox.

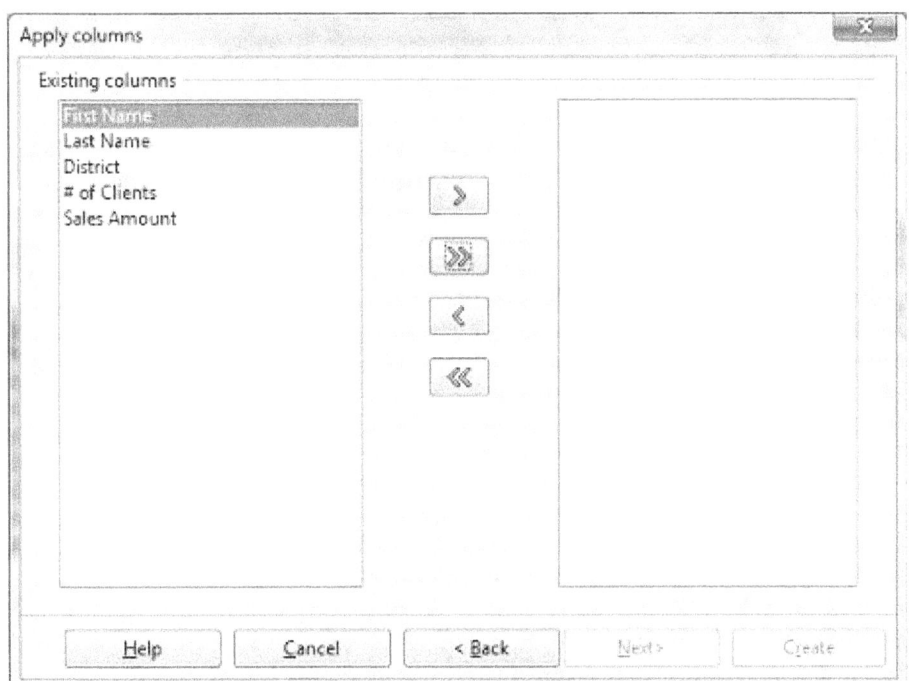

Figure 10

43

Step 11: This page of the Importing process allows users to choose which of the highlighted fields will be imported into the Base table. Using the left mouse button, highlight the desired fields and click the arrow buttons to move them to the right window.

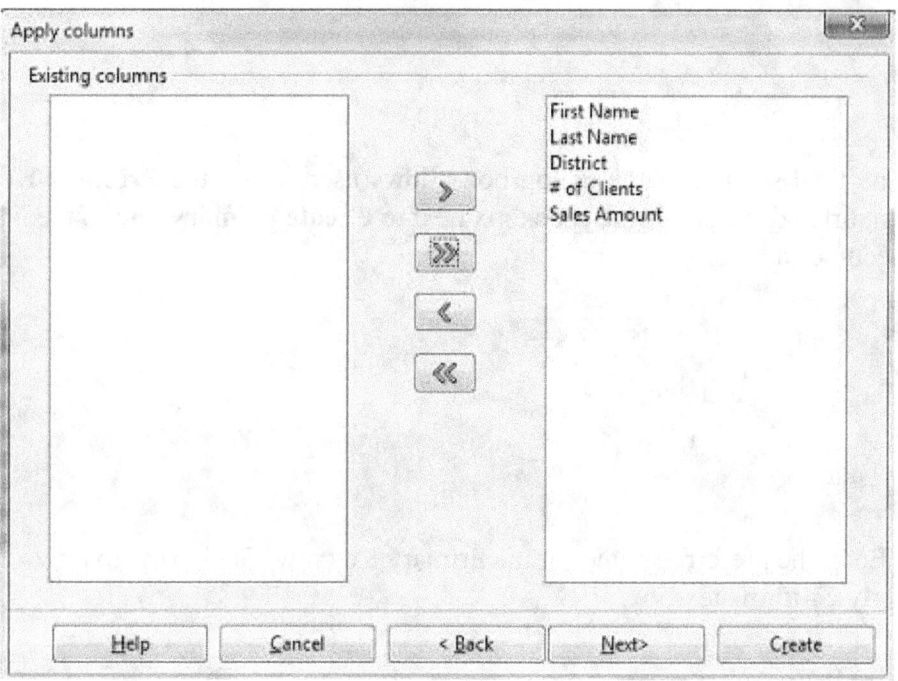

Figure 11

Step 12: Once the necessary fields have been moved to the right side of the **Apply columns** window, click **Next**. The **Type formatting** dialog box will appear.

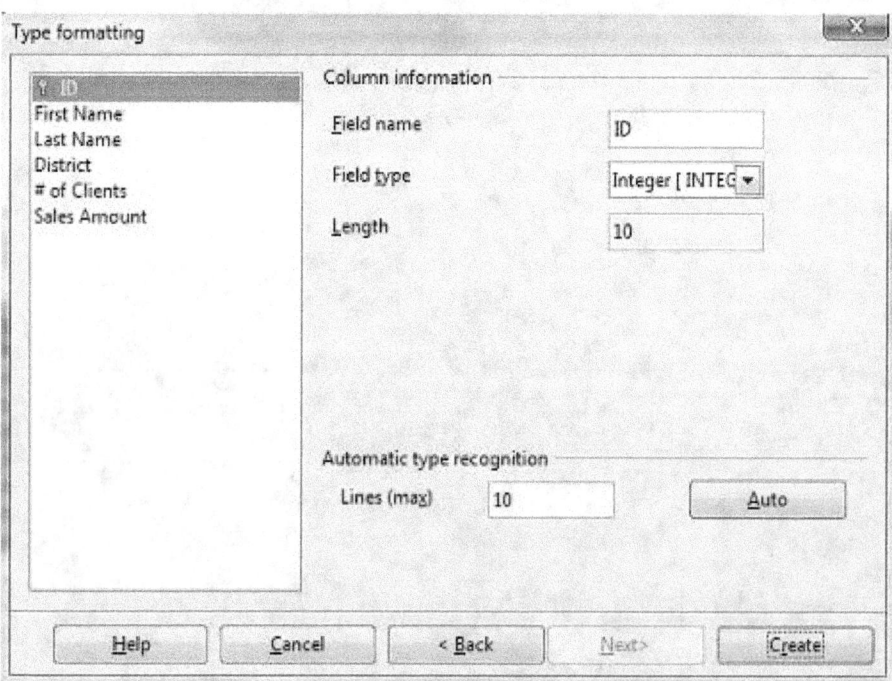

Figure 12

44

Step 13: In the Type Formatting window, enter the preferred Field name and Field type for the fields being imported.

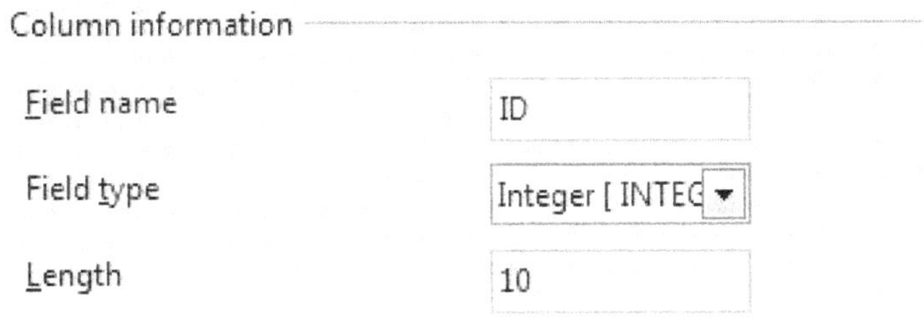

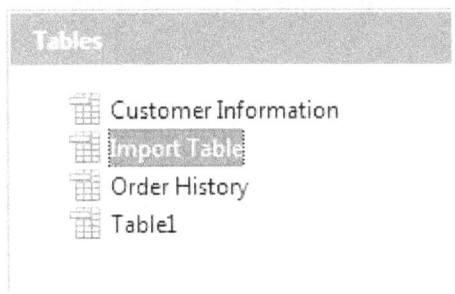

Figure 13

Step 14: Once all of the modifications have been made, click the **Create** button to finish the importing process. The data will now be available as a table within the Base database.

Figure 14

Growth & Assessment

1. Base allows users to import data from other applications and insert it into a database.

    a. TRUE

    b. FALSE

2. What button is selected when finished making changes within the Type Formatting window?

3. Why is the ability to import data from other applications and insert it into a database important?

Section 1.15 – Exporting Database Data

Section Objective:

- Learn how to export database data.

Exporting Data

OpenOffice Base allows users to export or move data into other applications in the OpenOffice Suite. This can be useful if a user wants to move of data into a Calc spreadsheet to perform calculations, or move the data into a Writer document to accompany a paper. The following steps outline how users can export Base data into other applications in the OpenOffice Suite.

Exporting into a Writer Document

Step 1: Create a new blank Writer document.

Step 2: Click **View** on the Menu Bar.

Step 3: From the View drop-down menu, select **Data Sources**. The **Data Sources** pane will appear above the document with a list of previously created databases.

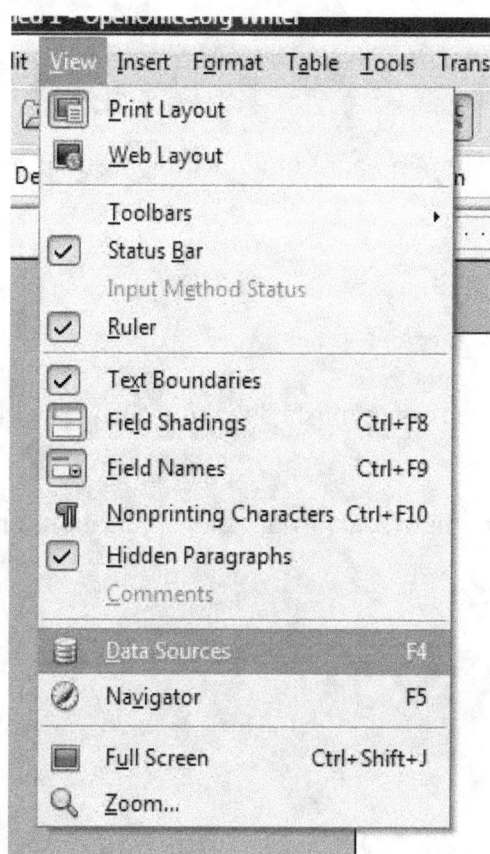

Figure 1

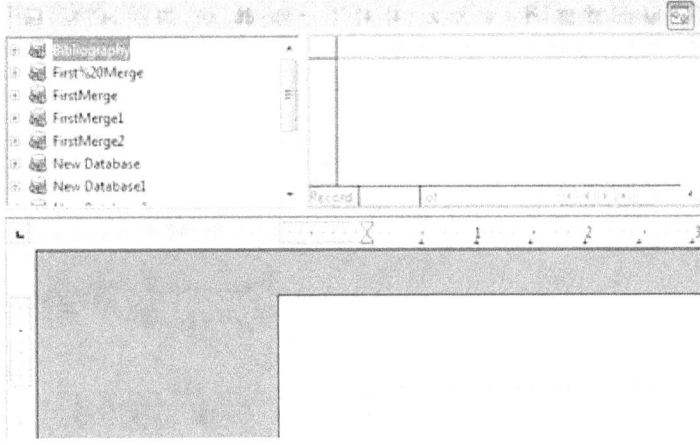

Figure 2

Step 4: Expand the database to select the table in which the data will be obtained.

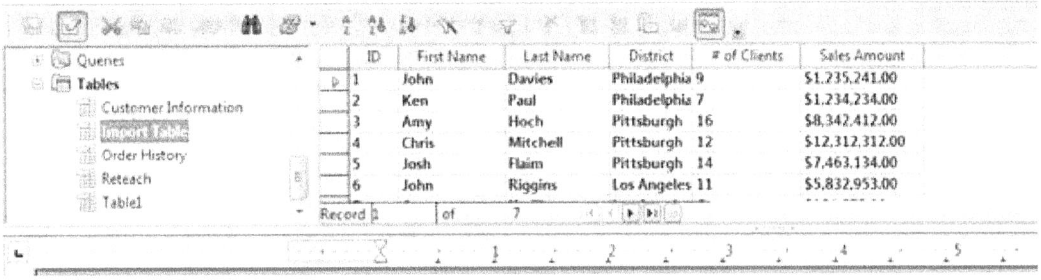

Figure 3

Step 5: From the selected table, highlight the desired data which will be exported into the Writer document.

Step 6: Using the left mouse button, click and hold the highlighted text. While holding the left mouse button, drag the cursor into the text document. Once the cursor is positioned over the document, release the left mouse button. The **Insert Database Columns** window will appear.

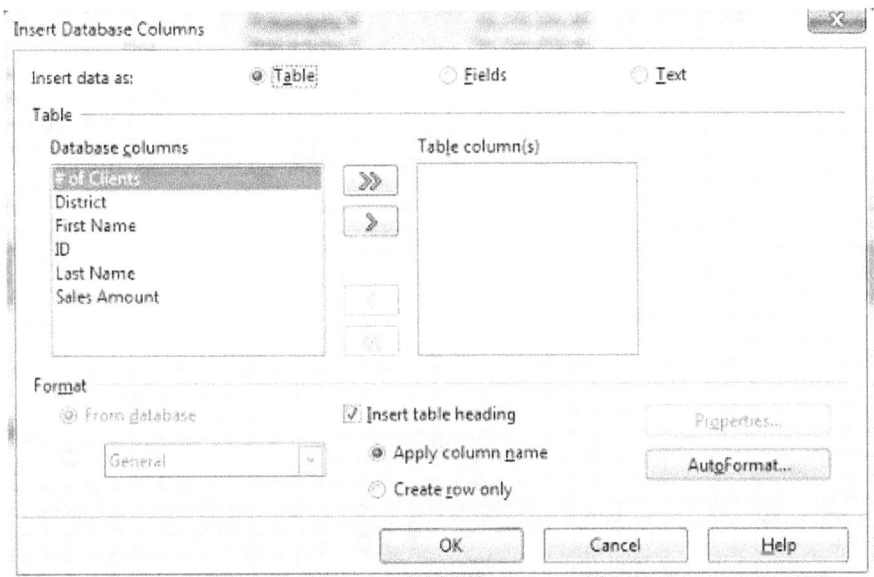

Figure 4

Step 7: Within the window, leave **Table** selected, and click the **>>** button to move all desired fields to the right side of the window.

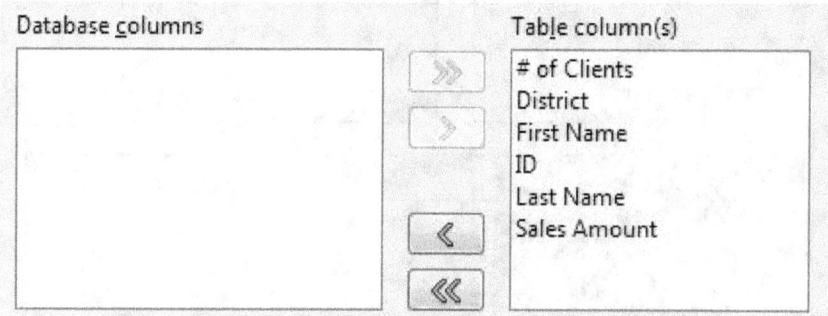

Figure 5

Step 8: Click **OK**. A table containing the selected information will be inserted into the Writer document.

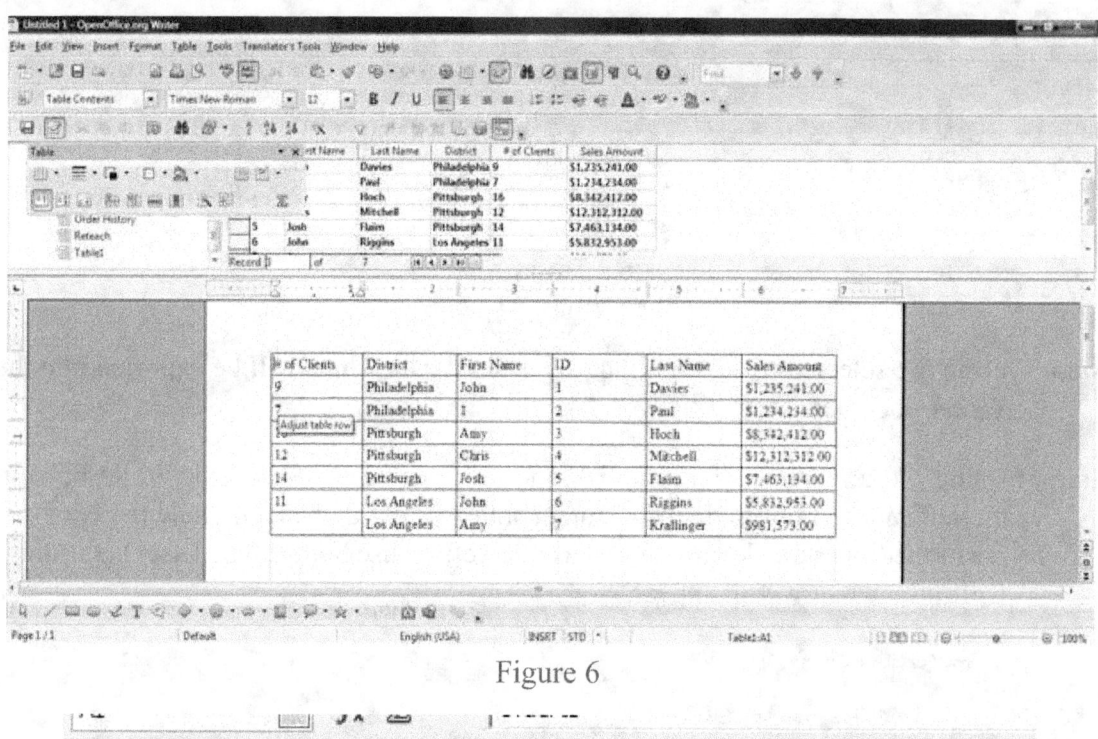

Figure 6

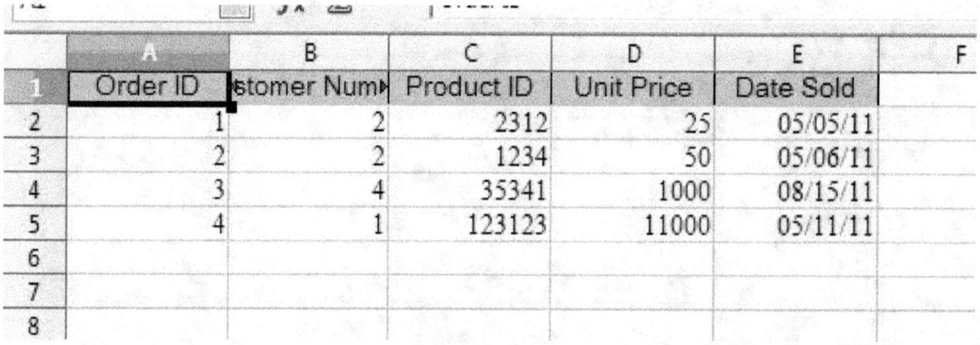

Figure 7

Exporting into a Calc Spreadsheet

Step 1: In Base, open an existing database table and highlight the entire table, including the headings.

Step 2: Click **Edit**, located on the Menu Bar.

Step 3: From the Edit drop-down menu, select **Copy**.

Step 4: Create a new blank Calc spreadsheet.

Step 5: Within the spreadsheet, select cell **A1**.

Step 6: Click **Edit**, located on the Calc Menu Bar.

Step 7: From the Edit drop-down menu, select **Paste**. The data from the Base table will be inserted into the Calc spreadsheet.

> **Note** – If some of the data doesn't fit in the default Calc column, resize the column width to view all of the data.

Growth & Assessment

1. Users are unable to resize the columns to view all of the data.

    a. TRUE

    b. FALSE

2. What happens when users click the >> buttons?

3. After highlighting and dragging new data from another document into a spreadsheet, what window will appear?

Unit Two

Section 2.1 – Common Database Terms   52

Section 2.2 – Using Edit, Delete, and Rename From the Toolbar   54

Section 2.3 – Creating a Form Using the Form Wizard   59

Section 2.4 – Using a Switchboard   65

Section 2.5 – Refining Form Properties   72

Section 2.6 – Modifying Fields in a Form   76

Section 2.7 – Using the Custom Color Menu   80

Section 2.8 – Refining a Form   84

Section 2.9 – Creating a Split Form   86

Section 2.10 – Adding Controls to Forms   89

Section 2.11 – Adding Controls Using the Control Wizard   93

Section 2.12 – Modifying the Layout of Fields on a Form   98

Section 2.13 – Creating a Relationship Between Tables   102

Section 2.14 – Adding a Subform Using the Form Wizard   105

Section 2.15 – Adding Symbols and Special Characters   111

Section 2.1 – Common Database Terms

Section Objective:

- Learn the following terms from Base: database application, controls, label controls, option buttons, and command buttons.

Understanding Terms in Base

Before a user begins to add additional parts to a Base database, certain terms need to be covered in order to better understand the application's features. The following terms should be learned before performing more advanced tasks in OpenOffice Base.

Database Application – A Database Application is a collection of records or data. It is a carefully structured catalog of information.

Controls – Controls are buttons, links, lists, and other pieces of user interface that can be added to forms. With these controls, a user can click a button to go to different parts of the database. Controls are similar to a Hyperlink.

Label Controls – A label is a control that displays static text, which means the text cannot be changed. Labels are most often used to display the name of a field, but they have many other uses as well, such as:

- The name of an unbound control

- The form subtitle (this should go in the Form Header section, below the title)

- Explanatory text (instructions for filling out the form, shortcut keys, etc…)

Option Buttons – An option button is a frame that can contain checkboxes, toggle buttons, and option buttons on a form, report, or database page. Users can use an option button to present alternatives from which users can select a single option.

Command Buttons – Command buttons provide users with a way of performing actions by clicking them. When the button is selected, it not only carries out the appropriate action, it also looks as if it's being pushed. A switchboard would be an example of a Command Button.

Growth & Assessment

1. What is a Database application?

2. What are Controls?

3. An Option Button is a frame that can contain check boxes, toggle buttons, and option buttons on a form, report, or database page.

    a. TRUE

    b. FALSE

4. What are Command Buttons?

Section 2.2 – Using Edit, Delete, and Rename From the Toolbar

Section Objective:

- Learn how to Edit, Delete, and Rename database objects using the Toolbar.

Using the Toolbar

In OpenOffice Base, the objects (Tables, Forms, Reports, and Queries) created for a database will change over time, as data is collected. Users will need to update the content and layout of the objects to reflect changes made to the database. When working in Base, users may find that an object, such as a query, is no longer needed and needs to be deleted. Tables and forms may also need to be modified and/or renamed so they reflect the data.

All of these changes can be done through the Base Toolbar. This section will explain the steps necessary to edit, delete, and rename database objects.

Before following the steps below, create a new Base database and insert data into a table as shown in the figure below.

Customer Number	First Name	Last Name	City	State
1	Amy	Mitchell	Pittsburgh	PA
2	Bob	Salzer	Philadelphia	PA
3	Ryan	Dunn	Chester	PA
4	John	Davies	Bedford	PA

Figure 1

Editing the Layout and Content of an Object

Step 1: From the main Base window, click on the **Tables** icon in the **Database** pane.

Figure 2

Step 2: Use the left mouse button to click and highlight the desired table.

Step 3: To make changes to the layout and design of the table, the table needs to be opened in **Design View**. To open the table in Design View, click the **Edit** button on the Toolbar. This will cause the table to open in Design View.

Figure 3

Figure 4

Step 4: To make changes to the actual content of the table, the table needs to be opened in **Data View**. To open the table in Data View, click on the **Open Database Object** button on the Toolbar. This will cause the table to open in Data View.

Figure 5

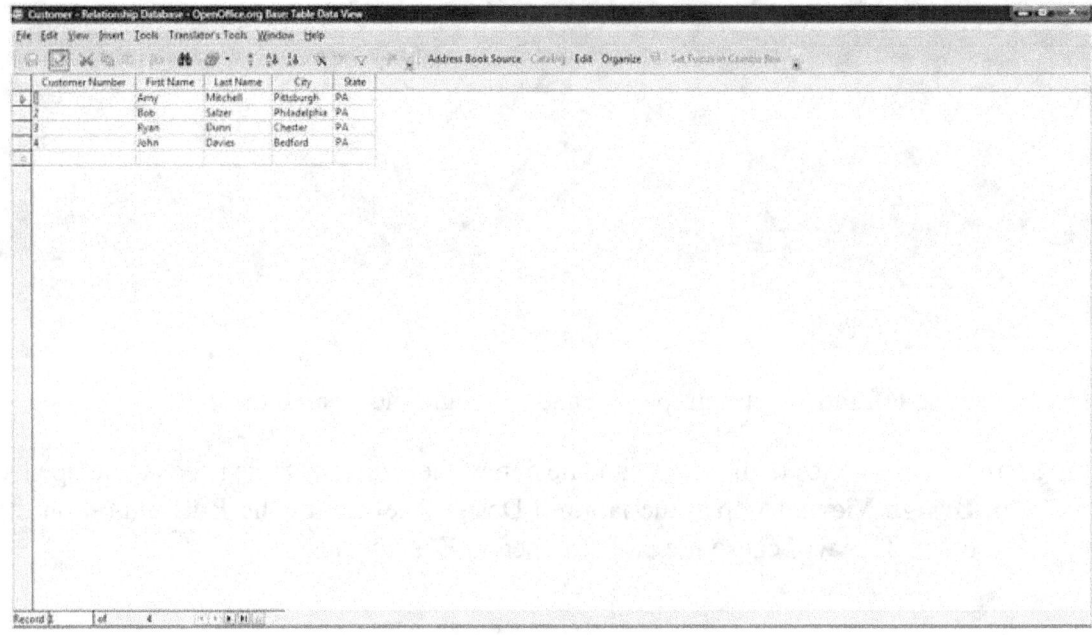

Figure 6

Renaming an Object

Step 1: From the main Base window, click on the **Tables** icon in the **Database** pane.

Step 2: Use the left mouse button to click and highlight the **Lesson 2** table.

Step 3: Click the **Rename** button on the Toolbar. The **Rename to** dialog box will appear.

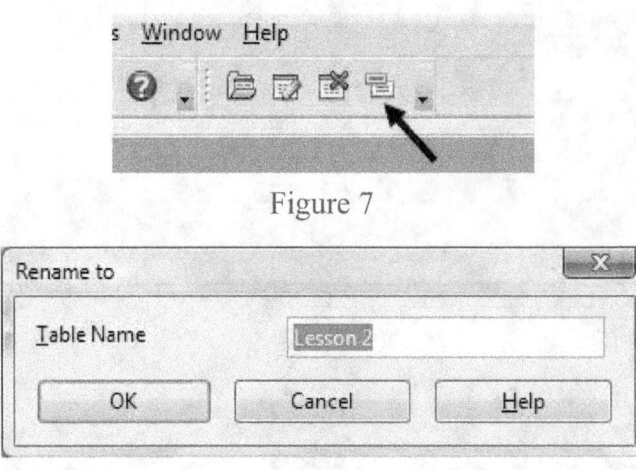

Figure 7

Figure 8

Step 4: Rename the table "**Rename Lesson 2**" and then click **OK**. The name change will instantly be made to the table.

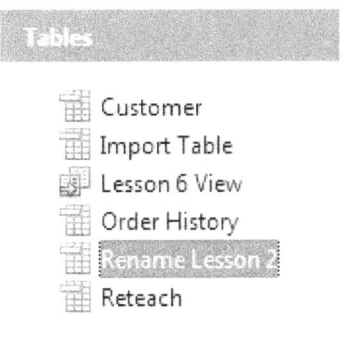

Figure 9

Deleting an Object

Step 1: From the main Base window, click on the **Tables** icon in the **Database** pane.

Step 2: Use the left mouse button to click and highlight the "**Rename Lesson 2**" table.

Step 3: Click the **Delete** button on the Toolbar.

Figure 10

Step 4: A confirmation pop-up will open and ask the user to confirm that the object should be deleted.

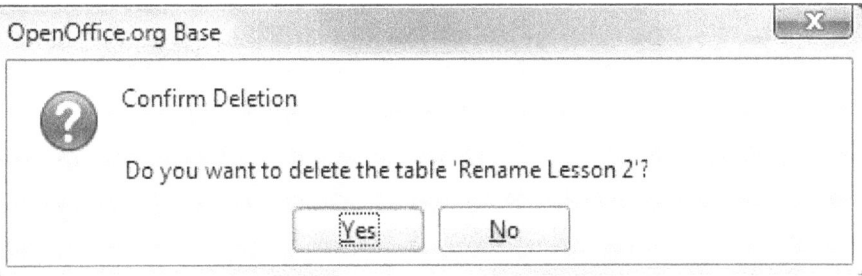

Figure 11

Step 5: Click the **Yes** button. The object will be removed from the database.

Note – The same steps can be applied to edit, rename or delete any of the object types found in OpenOffice Base.

Growth & Assessment

1. What should be selected in order to open the table in Data View?

2. The user will need to update the content and layout of the objects to reflect changes that are made to the data.

    a. TRUE

    b. FALSE

3. What opens after clicking the delete button on the toolbar?

Section 2.3 – Creating a Form Using the Form Wizard

Section Objective:

- Learn how to create a form using the Form Wizard.

The Form Wizard

OpenOffice Base allows users to create a Form by using the **Form Wizard**. Like other wizards, the Form Wizard provides a series of steps where various options can be applied to create the desired Form. The form that the wizard creates is a good starting point for further customization. The following steps outline how the Form Wizard can be accessed and used to create a Form in OpenOffice Base.

Step 1: Click on the **Forms** located on the **Database** pane.

Figure 1

Step 2: From the **Task** pane, select **Use Wizard to Create Form…**. The **Form Wizard** dialog box will appear.

Figure 2

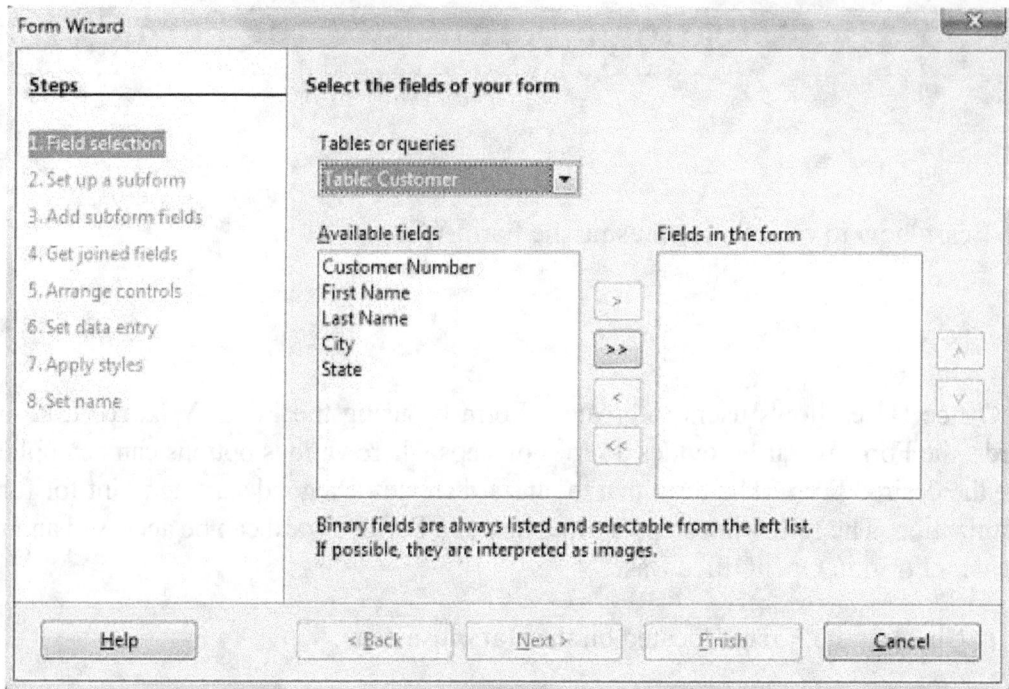

Figure 3

Step 3: Within the **Table or queries** portion of the dialog box, select the preferred table from the drop-down list.

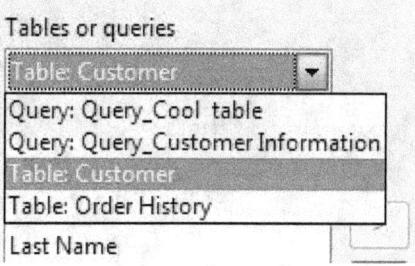

Figure 4

Step 4: In the **Available fields** window, highlight the fields that will be used in the form and then click the **>** button to move them into the **Fields in the form** window.

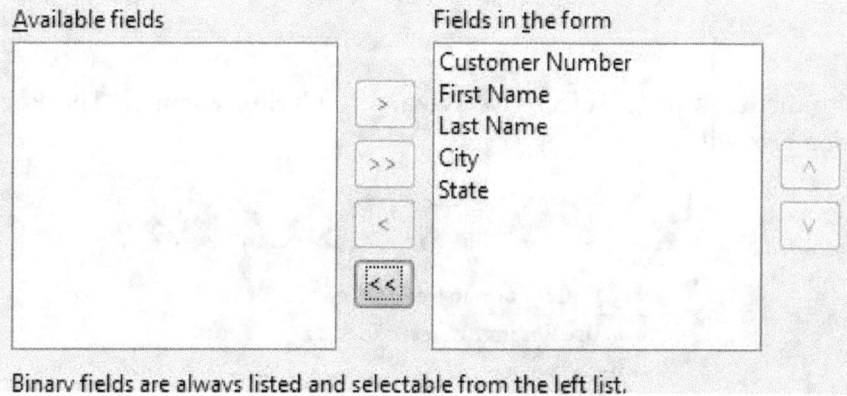

Figure 5

Step 5: Within the **Steps** pane, click on **5. Arrange controls** to display the corresponding step in the Wizard.

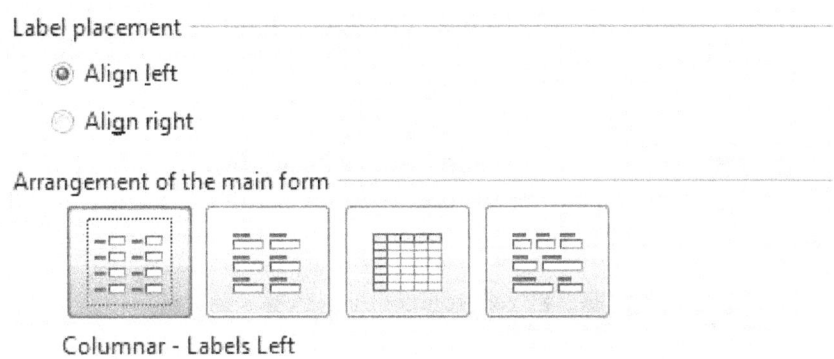

Figure 6

Step 6: The **Arrange controls** step is where users have the ability to choose how the form controls will be displayed on the screen. After selecting the layout, click the **Next** button to move to the next step in the wizard.

Figure 7

Step 7: The **Set Data Entry** step is where users decide whether the current data within the table will be carried over into the form, or if it will be blank. By default, the form will contain all of the data that was already found in the table. Select the preferred data and click **Next** to move to the next screen of the wizard.

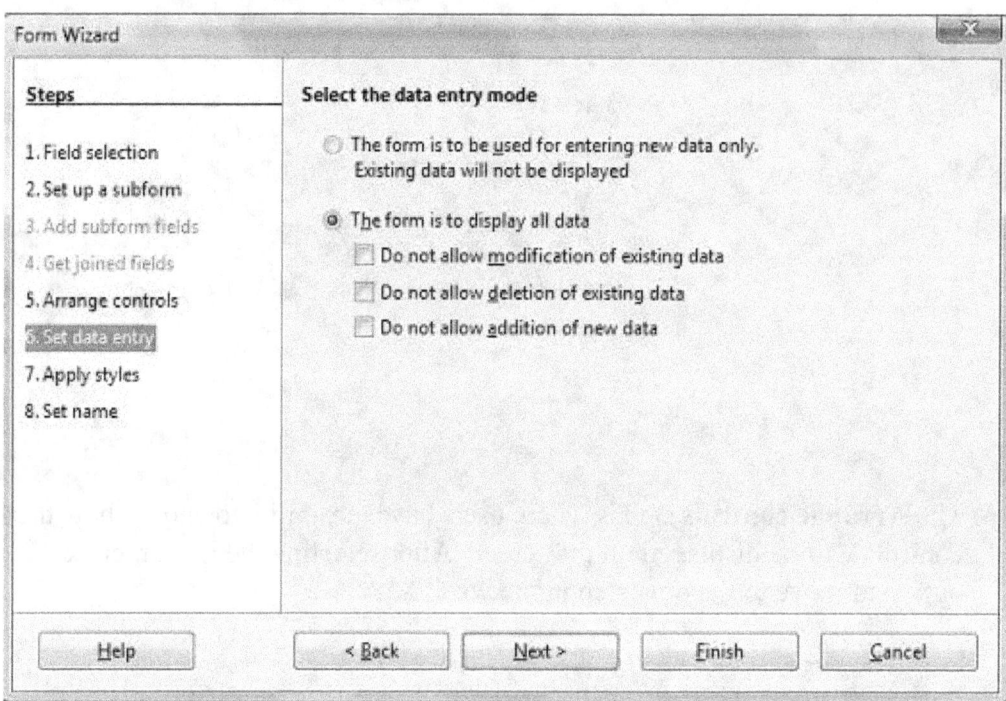

Figure 8

Step 8: The **Apply styles** window is where users can select a color for the background of the form. Users also have the ability to add a border. After making the necessary selections, click **Next** to move to the next screen.

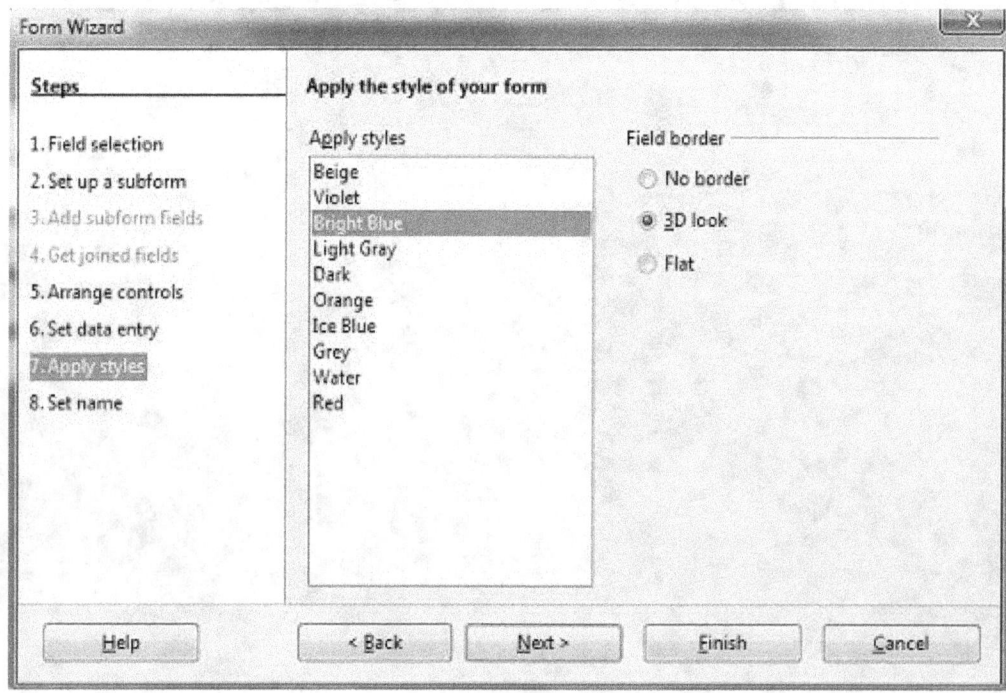

Figure 9

Step 9: The final screen of the wizard is the **Set name** screen. Here, users create a name for the form. Enter the preferred name into the textbox.

Set the name of the form

Name of the form

First Form

Figure 10

Step 10: From the Set name screen users have the ability to select how they want to work with the form once the wizard has finished it. Users will have two options to choose from, both are described below.

- **Work with the form** – This option will display the finished form and allow the user to begin entering data. This is similar to the Data view used with tables.

- **Modify the form** – This option will display the form and let the user manually move and format the controls contained in the form.

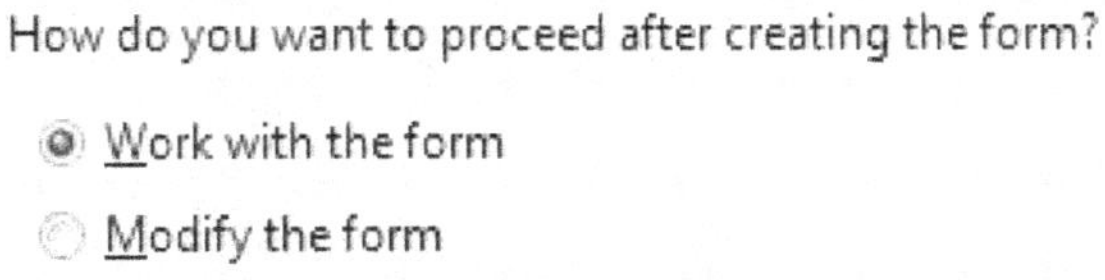

How do you want to proceed after creating the form?

◉ Work with the form

◯ Modify the form

Figure 11

Step 11: Click **Finish**. The created form will open displaying the first record found in the table that it is tied to.

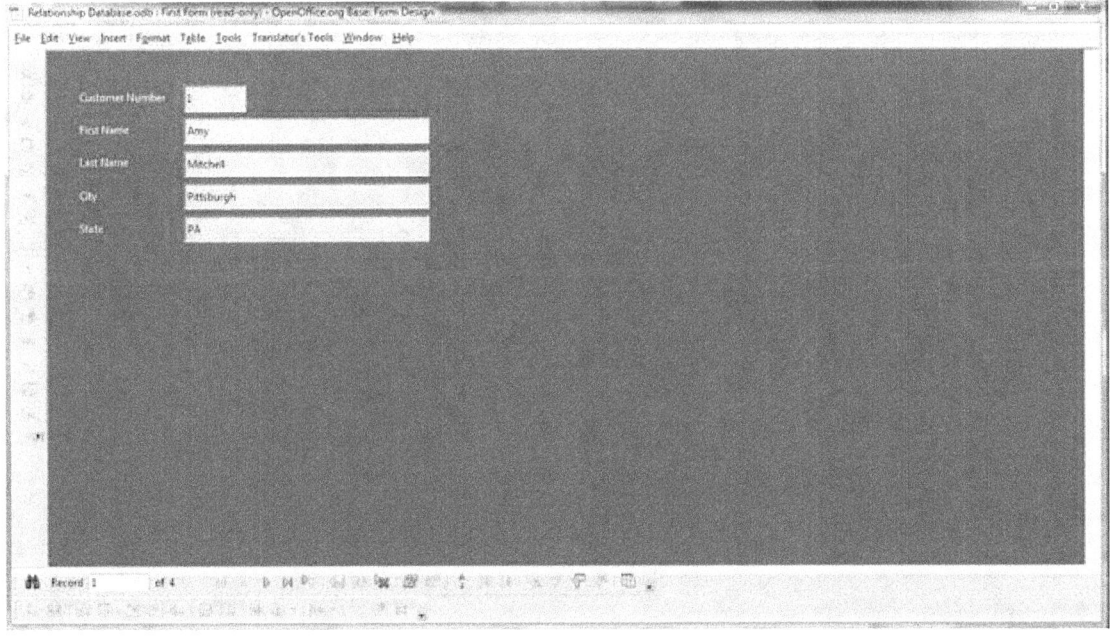

Figure 12

Growth & Assessment

1. What is the purpose of the Arrange controls step?

2. The Form Wizard is used to make forms.

    a. TRUE

    b. FALSE

3. The Work with the form option will display the form and let users manually move and format the controls contained in the form.

    a. TRUE

    b. FALSE

4. What is the purpose of the Apply styles window?

Section 2.4 – Using a Switchboard

Section Objective:

- Learn how to use a switchboard.

The Switchboard

A switchboard is an OpenOffice Base form that allows users to navigate through, or perform tasks within, the application. The form is essentially a customized menu that contains user-defined commands; buttons, labels, images, and/or hyperlinks which prompt actions that will automatically carry out tasks for the user. These tasks include, but are not limited to, opening other forms, running queries, or printing reports. This section will explain how to download the extension required to work with a switchboard, as well as learn how to create a switchboard that will direct the user to a form previously created.

Adding the Switchboard Extension

Step 1: Go to the following link: *http://extensions.services.openoffice.org/project/SwitchBoard*.

> **Note** – This link will navigate users to the OpenOffice.org **Extensions** website with the **Switchboard Extension** page displayed.

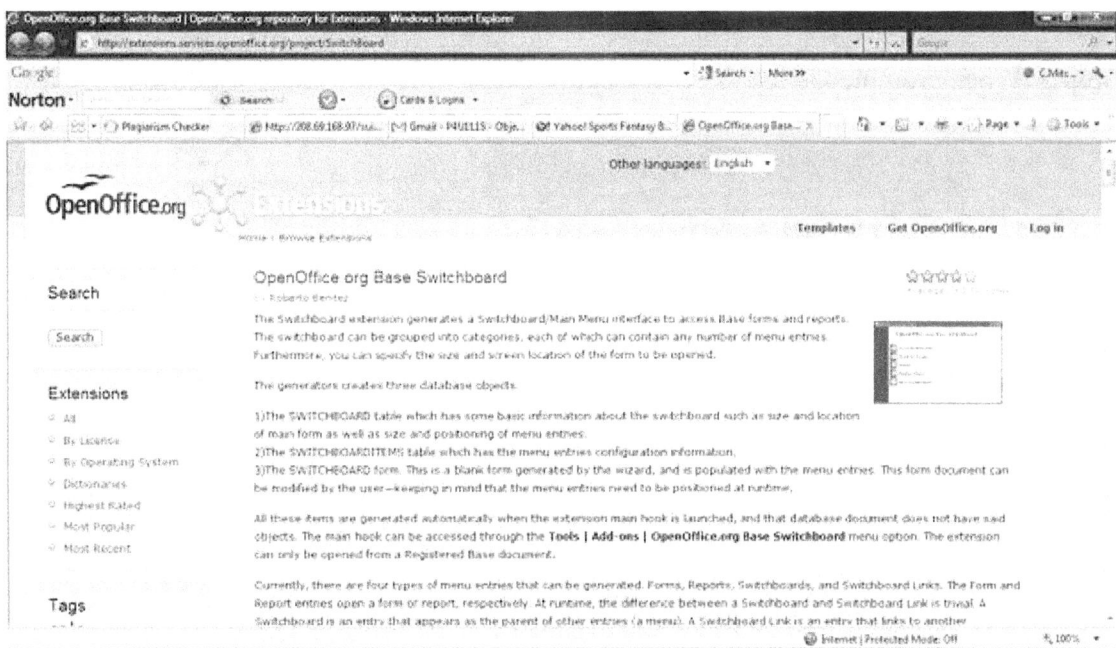

Figure 1

Step 2: Click on the **Get it!** button. This will direct the user to the **Download Page**.

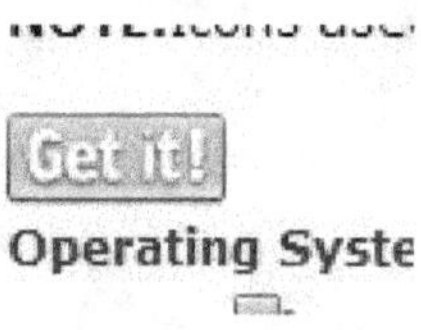

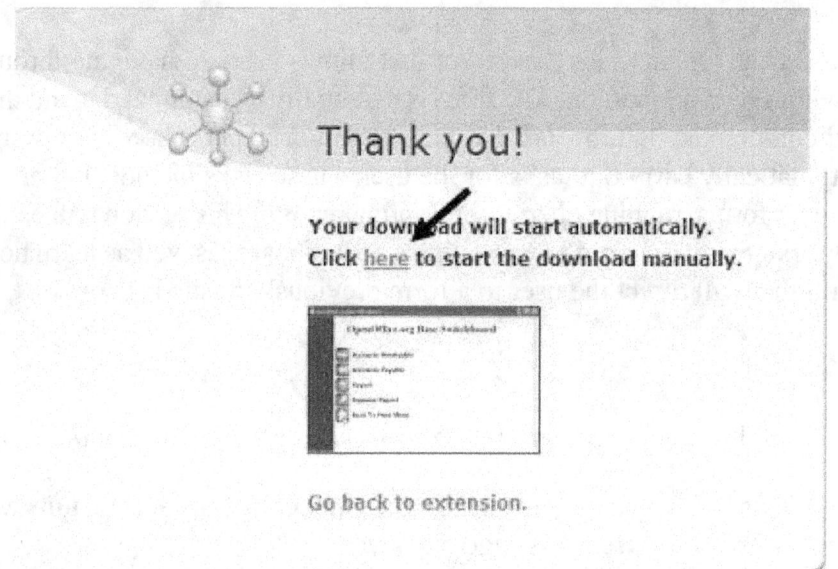

Figure 2

Step 3: Click on the **Manual Download** link to begin the downloading process.

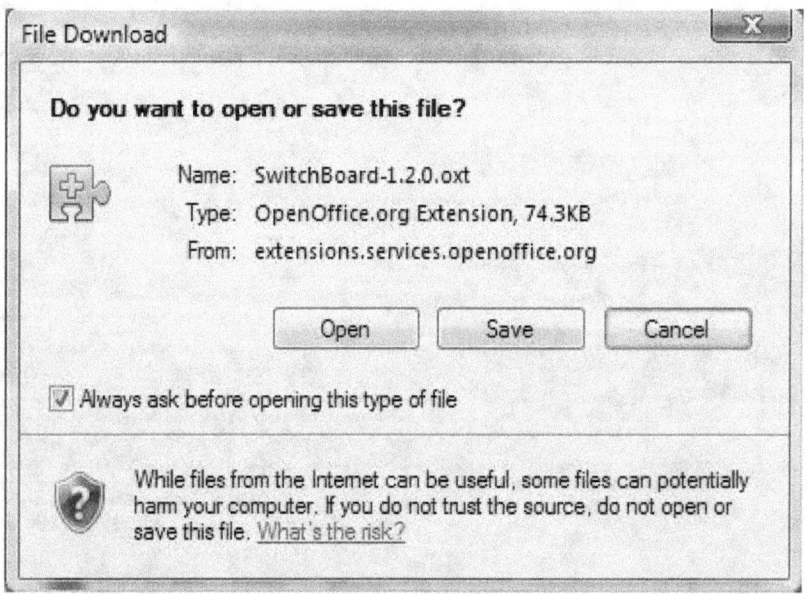

Figure 3

Step 4: When prompted, click the **Open** button on the File Download window.

Figure 4

Step 5: The next prompt will ask the user to verify the installation of the **Switchboard**. Click **OK**, and then click **Accept** to accept the license agreement.

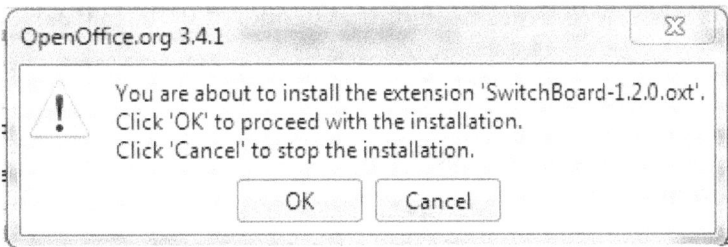

Figure 5

Step 6: After accepting the license agreement, the Extension Manager window will appear showing that the Switchboard has been added to Base. Click **Close** and the Switchboard can now be used in the application.

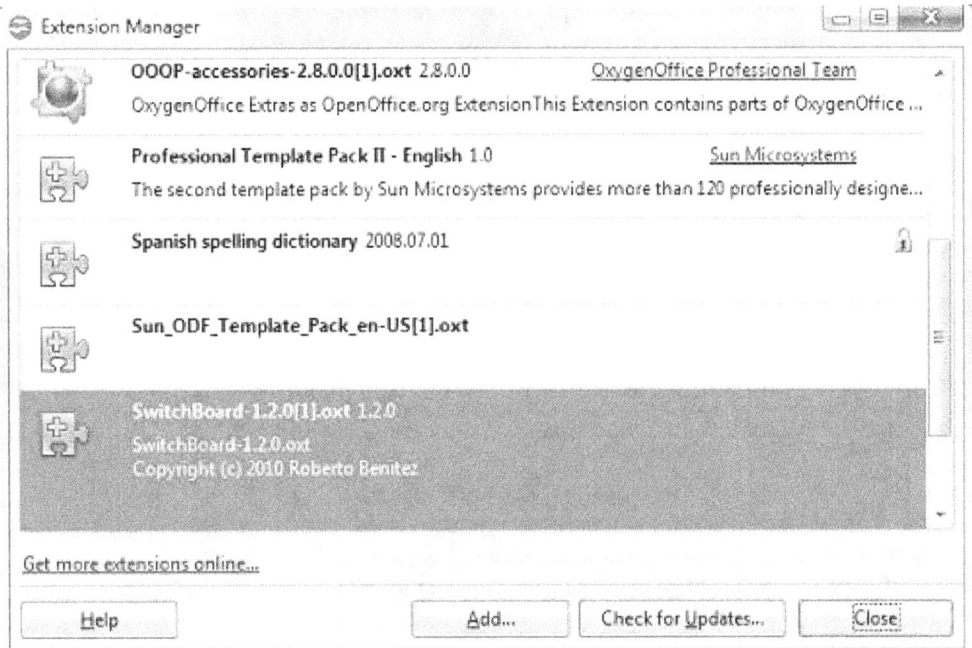

Figure 6

Using the Switchboard

Now that the extension necessary for installing the switchboard has been added, the user can follow the steps below to begin using the switchboard in the Base database.

Step 1: Create a new registered database.

Step 2: From the **Tools** drop-down menu, select **Add-Ons** and then select **OpenOffice Base Switchboard**.

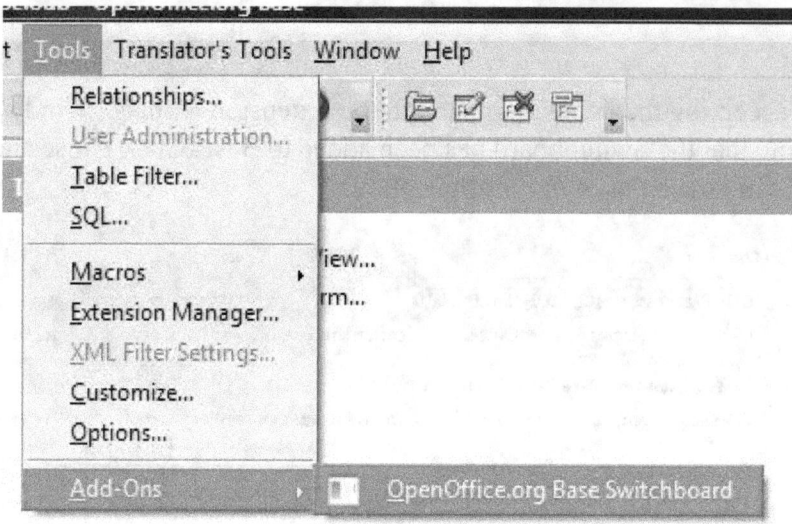

Figure 7

Note – A pop-up will appear informing the user that a form named **[Switchboard]** has not been created and that Base will create it for the user.

Figure 8

Step 3: The **Base Switchboard Creator** dialog box will open with the **Switchboard Settings** pane displayed. In the Main Title textbox, enter the preferred name. Once the name has been entered, use the nudge buttons to change the dimensions of the layout on the screen.

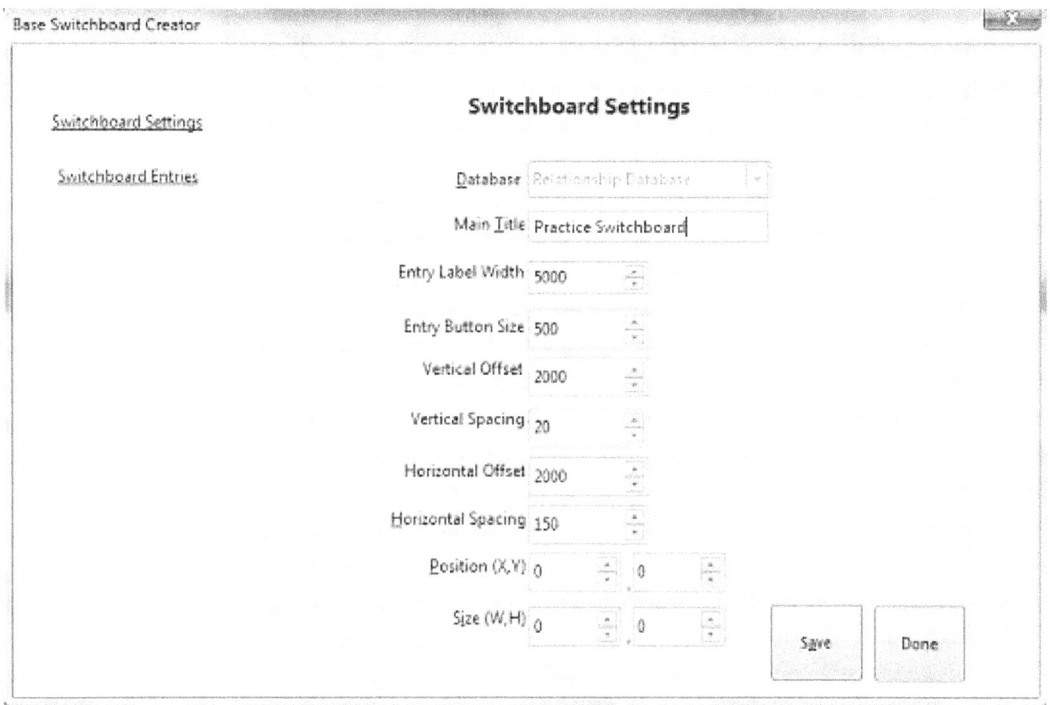

Figure 9

Step 4: Click the **Switchboard Entries** link, located on the left-hand side of the dialog box.

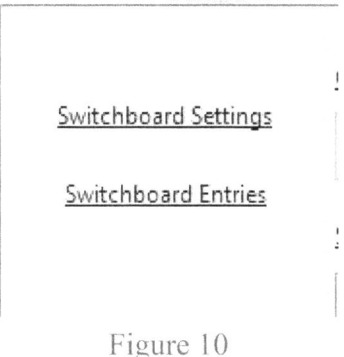

Figure 10

Step 5: The **Switchboard Entries** pane will appear. In the **Item Label** dialog box, type in the name of the switchboard.

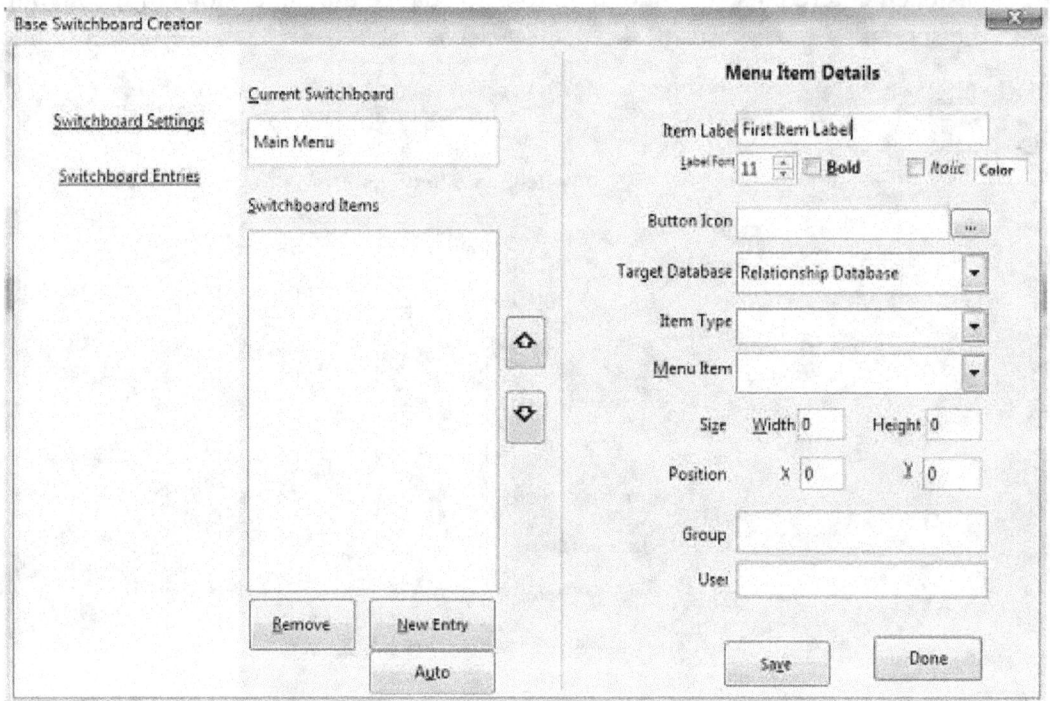

Figure 11

Step 6: In the **Target Database** pull-down menu, select the database created at the beginning.

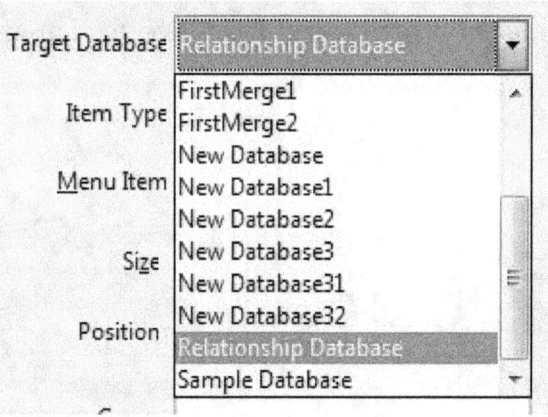

Figure 12

Step 7: In the **Item Type** pull-down menu choose **Switchboard**.

Figure 13

Step 8: Click **Save**. The new switchboard item will be entered into the textbox on the left-hand side of the pane.

Step 9: Click **Done**. The dialog box will close.

Step 10: Click on the **Forms** link in the Database pane of the main Base window. The Titled switchboard will be listed as one of the options.

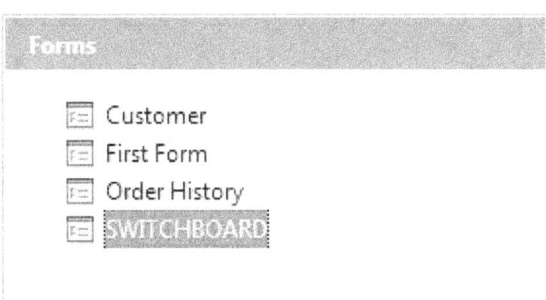

Figure 14

Step 11: Double-click on the titled link to open the switchboard. Here, the user can see the button created.

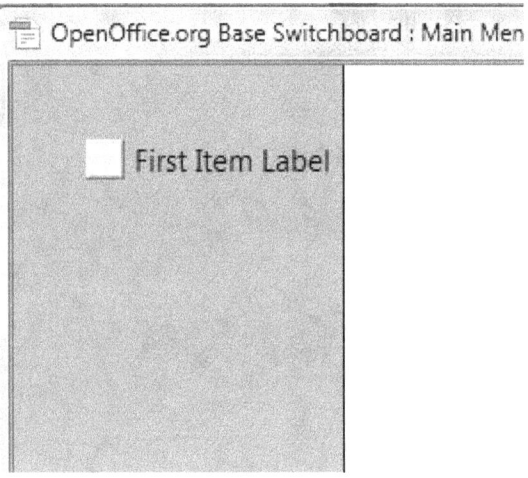

Figure 15

Growth & Assessment

1. What is a switchboard?

2. What does the switchboard allow the user to do?

3. What are some of the tasks switchboard can perform.

Section 2.5 – Refining Form Properties

Section Objective:

- Learn how to refine form properties.

Refining Form Properties

The **Form properties** feature in OpenOffice Base is used to determine a form's characteristics. The controls and sections on a form also have properties that determine the appearance, behavior, and structure of the control, as well as the data it contains. Form properties may be set with the property sheet. The following steps outline how this is done.

Step 1: Open an existing Base database that contains a form or, create a new database and create a form.

Step 2: Click on the **Forms** link located in the Database pane, and then right-click on a form so that the **Quick Menu** appears. Select **Edit** from the Quick Menu. The Form will open in Design view.

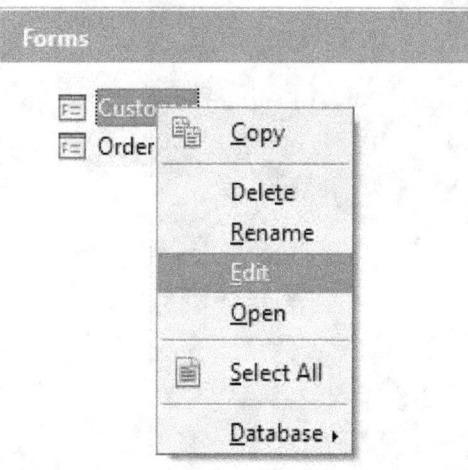

Figure 1

Figure 2

Step 3: Using the left mouse button, click and drag the cursor over any control found within the form so that it is highlighted.

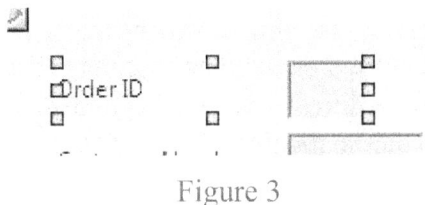

Figure 3

Step 4: Right-click the highlighted controls to make the **Quick Menu** appear. From the Quick menu, select **Control…**. The **Properties** dialog box will appear.

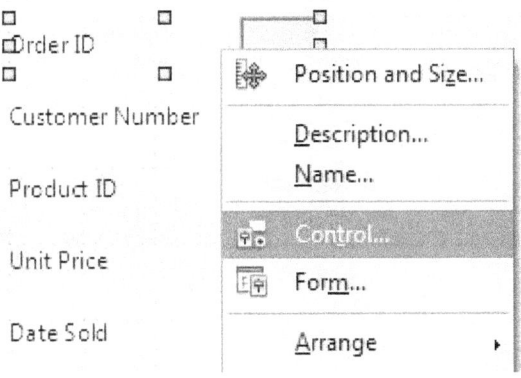

Figure 4

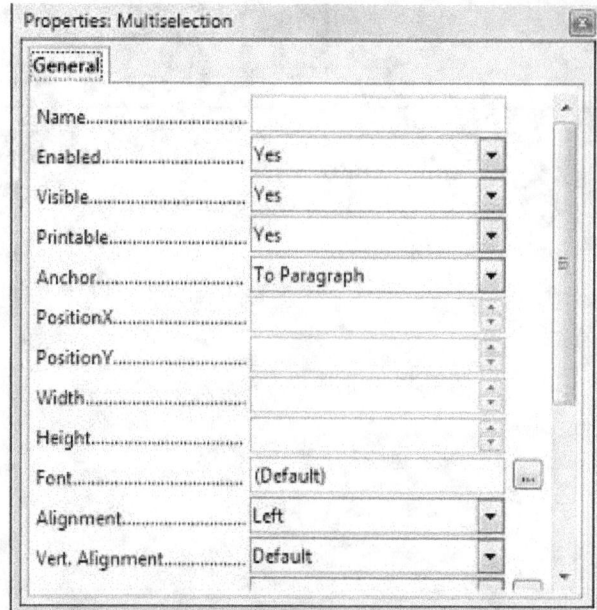

Figure 5

Step 5: In the **Properties** dialog box, users have the ability to modify the settings of the property boxes that display a downward pointing arrow. Background color is just one of many settings users can modify. View the available options by clicking the down-arrow and accessing the drop-down menu of predefined settings. Here, users may also enter the desired expression or setting directly into the property box. Once all of the desired modifications have been made, close the dialog box and the changes will be saved automatically.

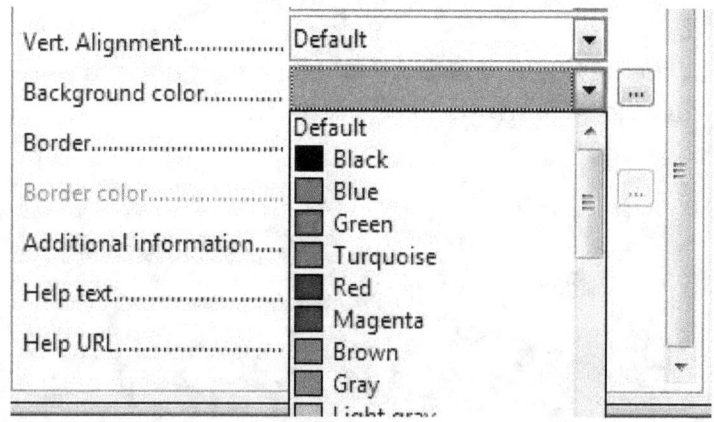

Figure 6

Growth & Assessment

1. Form Properties in OpenOffice Base is used to determine a form's characteristics.

    a. TRUE

    b. FALSE

2. What can form properties be set with?

3. Background color is one of the many modifiable settings.

    a. TRUE

    b. FALSE

4. What appears after selecting Control… from the Quick Menu?

Section 2.6 – Modifying Fields in a Form

Section Objective:

- Learn how to modify the font, size, and color of fields in a form.

Modifying Fields

In OpenOffice Base, modifying the font, color, and size of the data entered into the database form controls, is not allowed. The application does this to reduce user error; however, in the database form fields, Base removes these restrictions and allows users to modify the fields. Users have the ability to modify the look of the text throughout an entire form, or change specific fields to make them appear different than the rest of the form. This section outlines the necessary steps for modifying the look of the text displayed in the Base form controls.

Step 1: Open an existing Base database form in Design View. Once opened, select any of the fields displayed in the form.

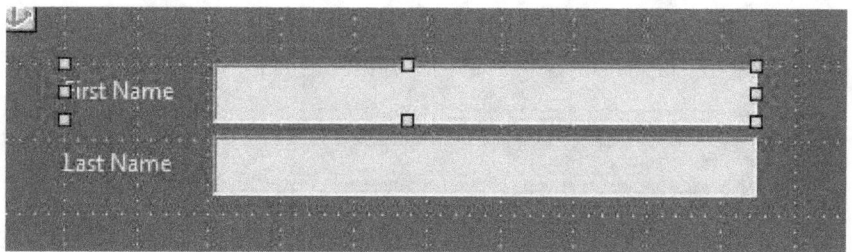

Figure 1

Step 2: Right-click the selected field to display the **Quick Menu**.

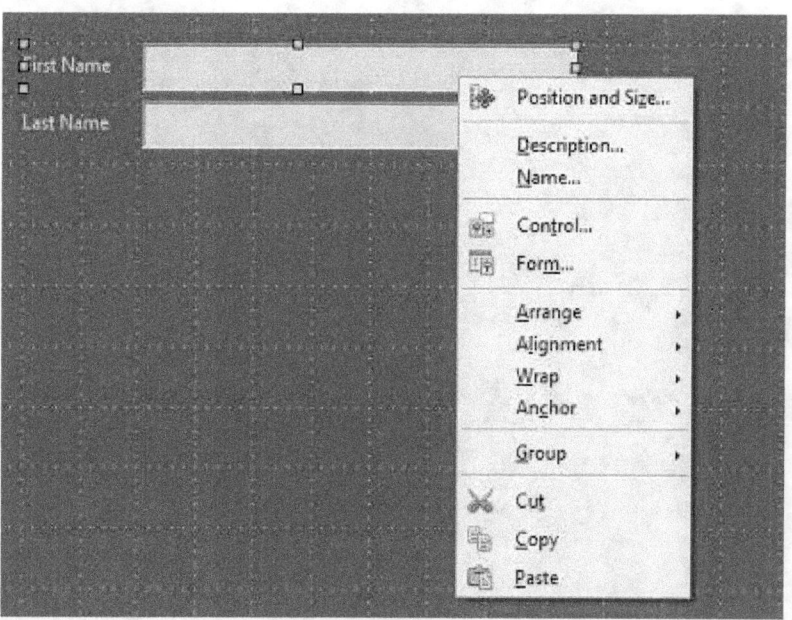

Figure 2

Step 3: From the Quick Menu, select **Control…**. The **Properties** dialog box will appear.

Figure 3

Step 4: In the Properties dialog box, scroll down to the **Font** option.

    Note – There will not be a value listed in the Font textbox.

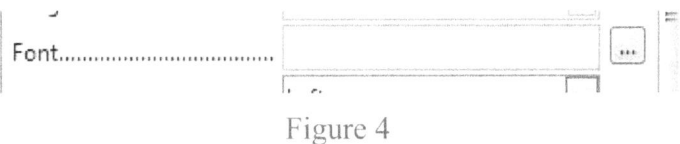

Figure 4

Step 5: Click the **Ellipsis** button "**…**" to the right of the Font textbox. The Character dialog box will appear.

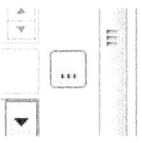

Figure 5

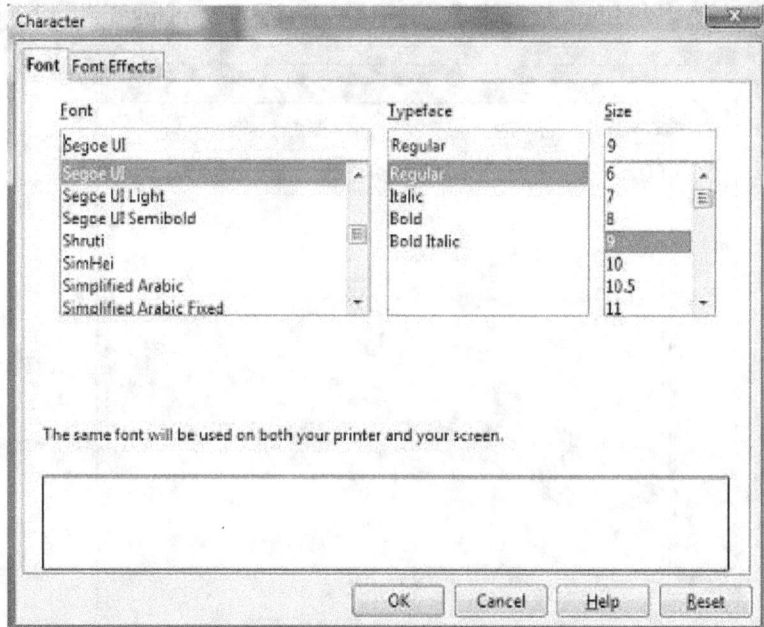

Figure 6

Step 6: Click the Font tab located at the top of the dialog box.

Step 7: From the **Font** scroll list, select the preferred font.

Step 8: From the **Size** scroll list, select the preferred font size.

Step 9: Click on the **Font Effects** tab.

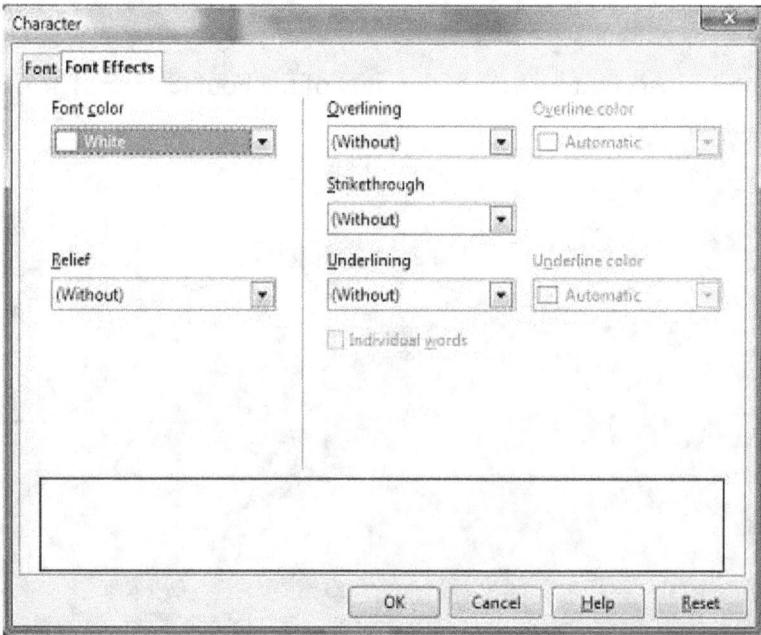

Figure 7

Step 10: In the **Font Color** drop-down menu, select the desired font color.

Step 11: Click **OK**. The Character dialog box will close, and the **Form** textbox will be updated based on the specified modifications.

Figure 8

Step 12: Close the **Properties** dialog box. The changes will be applied to the highlighted control.

Note – To change all the labels at once, press **CTRL + A** to select all of the fields on the form and then follow the steps provided above.

Growth & Assessment

1. What is the keyboard shortcut used to "select all"?

2. Why does Base not allow the user to modify form controls?

3. What does the ellipses button look like?

4. Modifying the font, color, and size of the data entered into the database form controls is allowed.

    a. TRUE

    b. FALSE

Section 2.7 – Using the Custom Color Menu

Section Objective:

- Learn how to use the Custom Color menu.

The Custom Color Menu

OpenOffice Base allows users to add color to the forms within a database. The Custom Color Menu provides many colors to choose from and allows users to customize the form color. This is helpful when trying to add visual appeal to the forms in Base. The following steps outline how to access and use the Custom Color Menu.

Step 1: Open a Form in **Design** view.

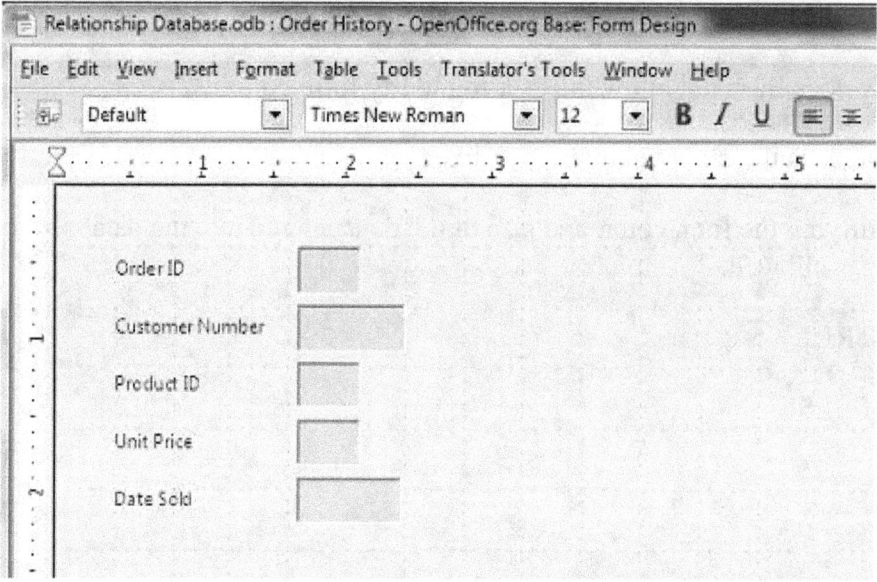

Figure 1

Step 2: Select any control so it is highlighted with a border around it.

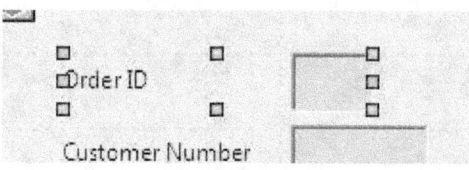

Figure 2

Step 3: Right-click the selected control. The Quick Menu will appear.

Step 4: From the Quick Menu, select **Control…**. The **Properties** dialog box will appear.

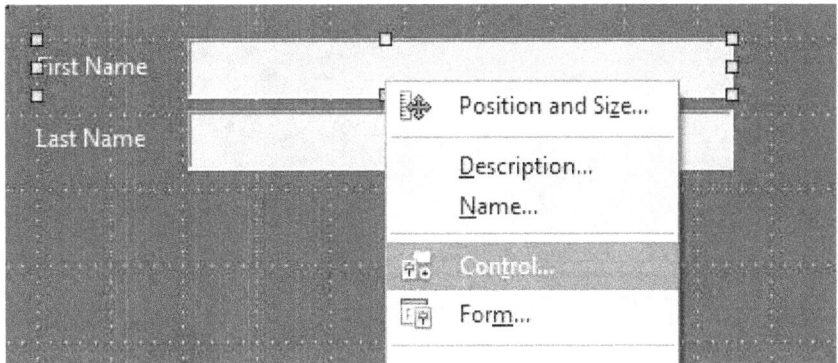

Figure 3

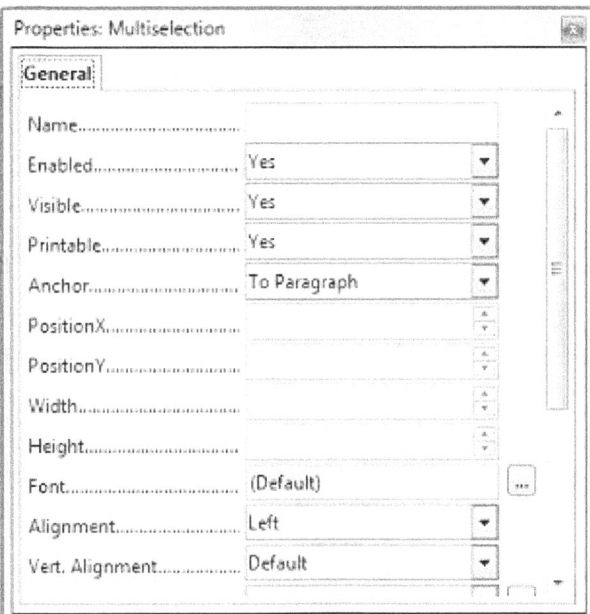

Figure 4

Step 5: Click the **Ellipse** button "**…**" next to the **Background Color** textbox. The **Color** dialog box will appear.

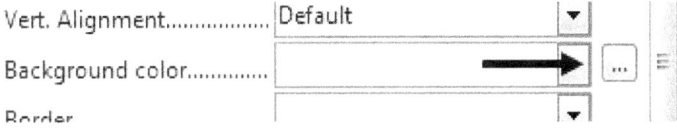

Figure 5

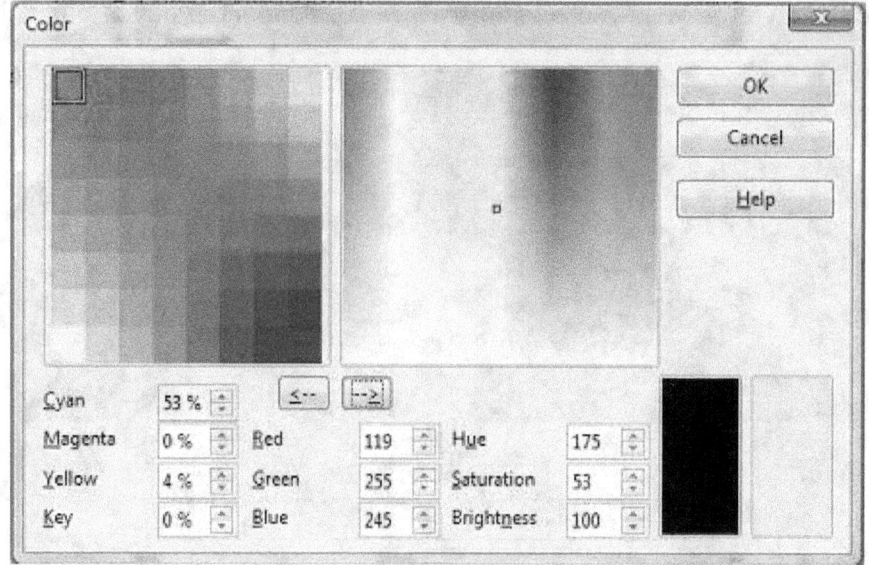

Figure 6

Step 6: On the right-hand side of the Color dialog box, click anywhere within the **Custom Color** box and hold the left mouse button and drag the cursor around the box to create a custom color.

Note – The two color boxes located on the bottom right-hand side of the dialog box will show the current color (the left box) and the new color (the right box).

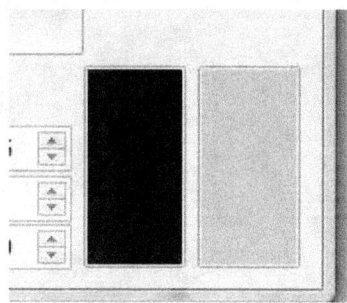

Figure 7

Step 7: Once the preferred color has been created, click the **OK**. The Color dialog box will close and the new color will be applied to the control.

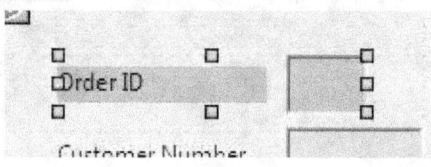

Figure 8

Step 8: Close the **Properties** dialog box to complete modifying the Control.

Growth & Assessment

1. OpenOffice Base allows the user to add color to the Forms within a database.

    a. TRUE

    b. FALSE

2. What is the purpose of the two color boxes found within the Color dialog box?

3. Why is adding color to a form important?

4. Clicking the ellipses button will open the Color dialog box.

    a. TRUE

    b. FALSE

Section 2.8 – Refining a Form

Section Objective:

- Learn how to refine a form by adding fields.

Refining a Form

In OpenOffice Base, users have the ability to modify a form's design by using the **Form Design** toolbar. The toolbar allows users to duplicate any fields within the form, or add a completely new field that was not originally included. The following steps outline how to use the Form Design toolbar to add a new field into a Base form.

Step 1: Open a form in **Design** view.

Step 2: Click **View** on the Menu Bar.

Step 3: From the **View** drop-down menu, scroll over **Toolbars** and select **Form Design**. The **Form Design** toolbar will appear horizontally on the bottom left-hand of the screen.

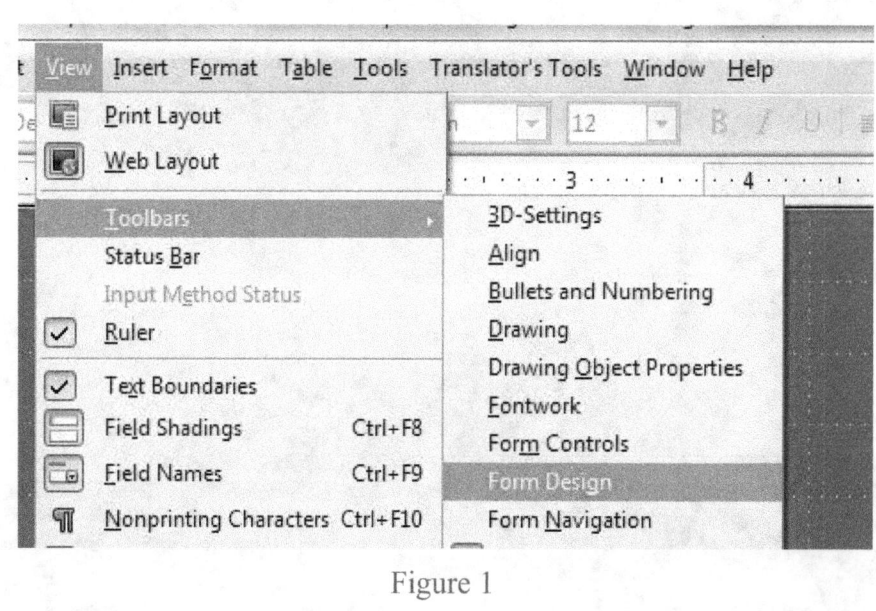

Figure 1

Figure 2

Step 4: Click on the **Add Field** button on the Form Design toolbar. The **Add Field** dialog box will appear.

Figure 3

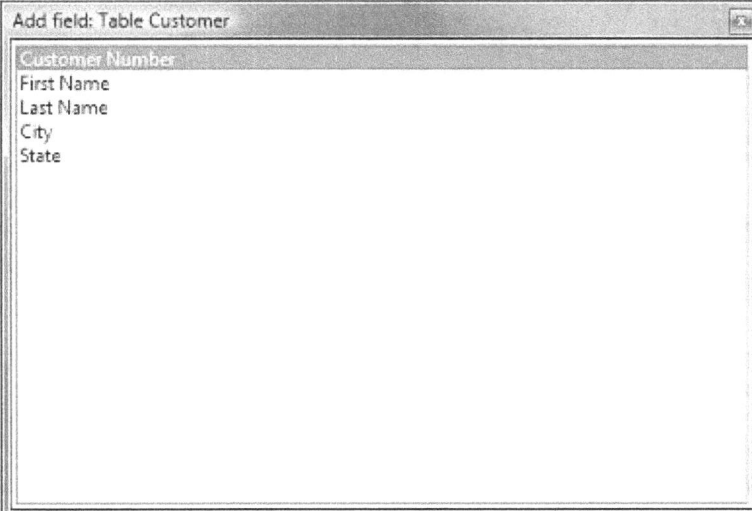

Figure 4

Step 5: Double-click on the desired fields to add them to the form. Once selected, the fields will be inserted into the form. Once all of the fields have been added, close the dialog box.

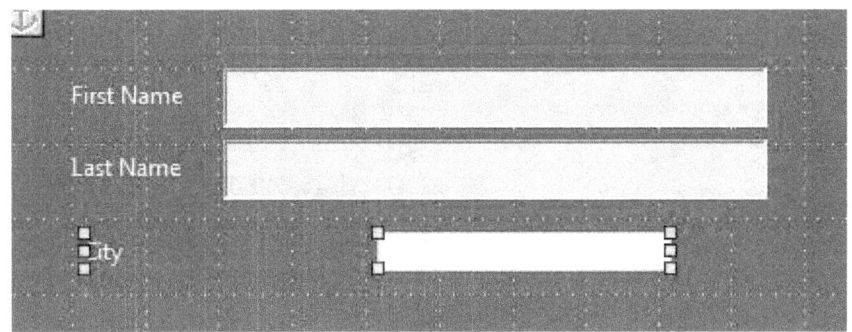

Figure 5

Step 6: Using the left mouse button, click and drag the fields that have been previously added to position them on the form. Once this has been done, the desired fields will be added to the preferred location on the form.

Growth & Assessment

1. What action would a user take once all of the fields have been added?

2. The toolbar does not allow users to duplicate any fields within the form, or add a completely new field that was not originally included.

    a. TRUE

    b. FALSE

3. What toolbar allows users to modify a form's design?

Section 2.9 – Creating a Split Form

Section Objective:

- Learn how to create a split form.

Creating a Split Form

In OpenOffice Base, a split form provides users with two views of the database at the same time; the top of the window shows the data as a **Table in Data** view, and the bottom of the window displays the original **Form**. The two views are connected to the same data source and are synchronized with each other at all times. Selecting a field in one part of the form selects the same field in the other part of the form. Users have the ability to add, edit, or delete data from either part of the split form. The following steps outline how to add a split form to an existing form.

Step 1: Create a new form in a Base database.

Order ID	Customer Number	Product ID	Unit Price	Date Sold
1	2	2312	25	05/05/11
2	2	1234	50	05/06/11
3	4	35341	1000	08/15/11
4	1	123123	11000	05/11/11

Figure 1

Step 2: Open the previously created form in **Data view**.

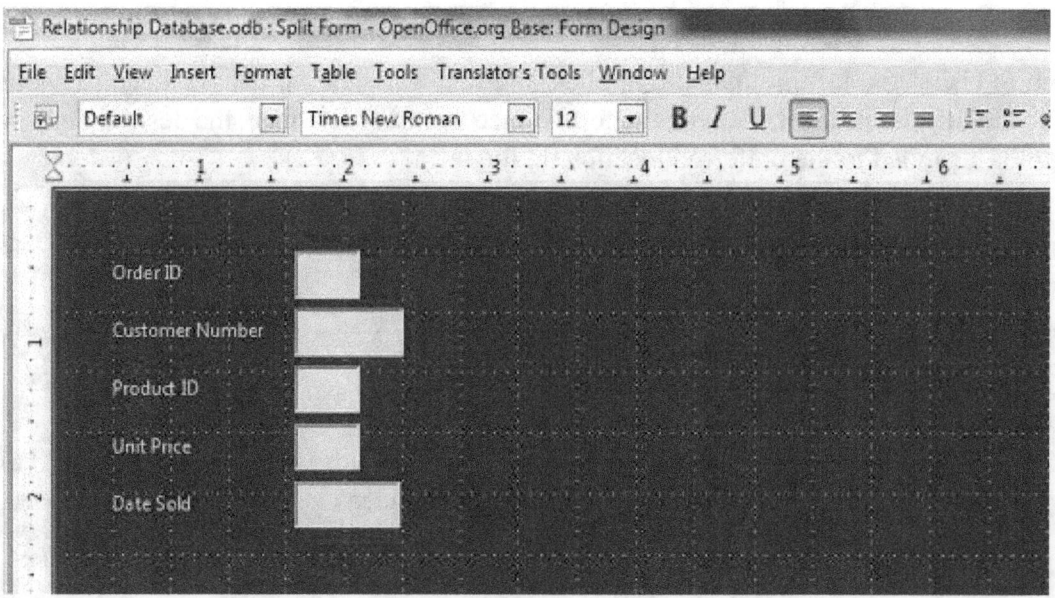

Figure 2

Step 3: Click **View**, located on the Menu Bar.

86

Step 4: From the **View** drop-down menu, scroll over **Toolbars** and select **Form Navigation**. The **Form Navigation** toolbar will appear horizontally on the bottom of the screen.

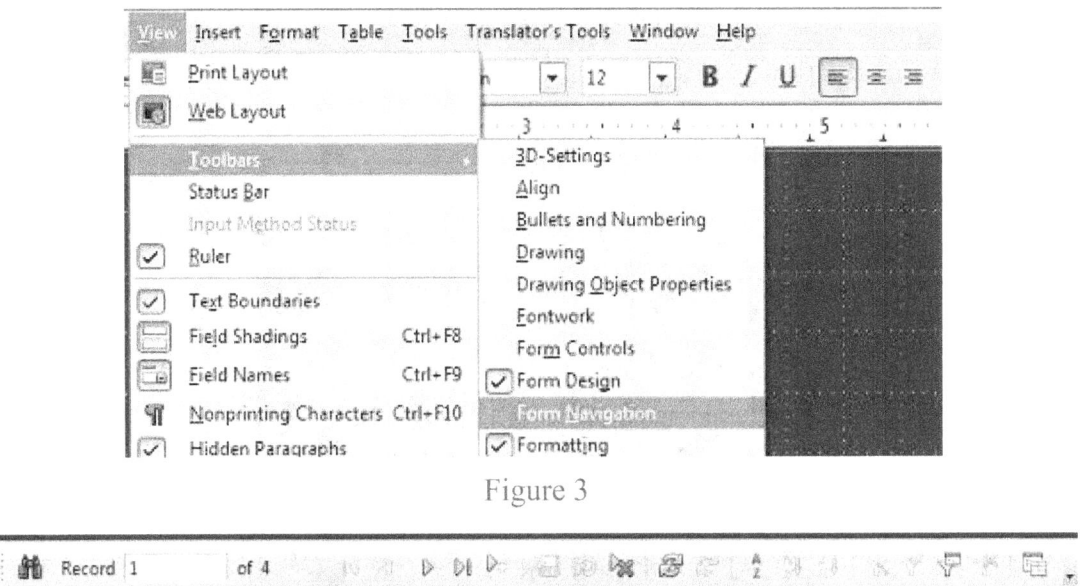

Figure 3

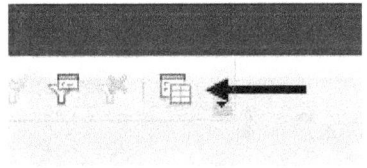

Figure 4

Step 5: Click on the **Data Source as Table** button, located on the right-hand side of the **Form Navigation** toolbar. A table containing the source information used to build the form will open above the form.

Figure 5

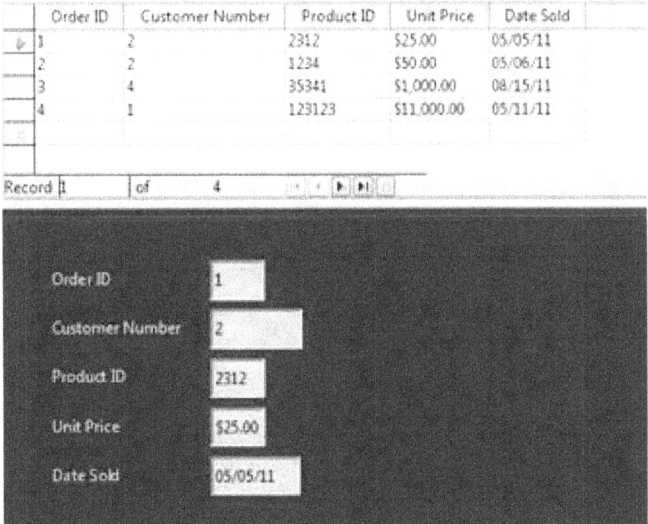

Figure 6

Step 6: Make the desired modifications to the table at the top of the screen. All of the changes will be reflected in the form below.

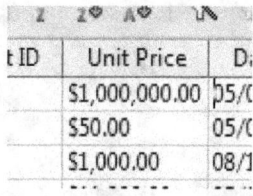

Figure 7

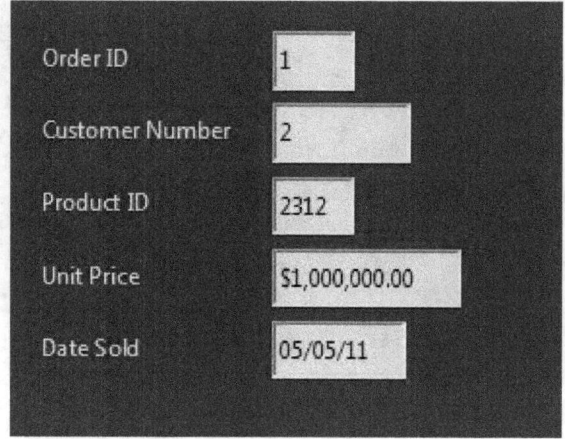

Figure 8

Note – If a user would like to hide the table and only view the form, click the **Data Source as Table** button again, which is located on the **Form Navigation** toolbar.

Growth & Assessment

1. What does the split view do?

2. What are the two views?

3. The two views are connected to the same data source and are synchronized with each other at all times.

    a. TRUE

    b. FALSE

4. The user does not have the ability to add, edit, or delete data from either part of the split form.

    a. TRUE

    b. FALSE

Section 2.10 – Adding Controls to Forms

Section Objective:

- Learn how to add controls to forms.

Adding Controls

In OpenOffice Base, controls are objects that display data, perform actions, and let users view and work with information that enhances users interface, such as labels and images. The most commonly used control is the textbox, but other controls include labels, checkboxes, and subform/subreport controls. The following steps explain how to add controls to a form.

Step 1: Open a form in **Design** view.

Step 2: Click **View**, located on the Menu Bar.

Step 3: From the **View** drop-down menu, scroll over **Toolbars** and select **Form Controls**. The **Form Controls** toolbar will appear vertically on the left-hand side of the application window.

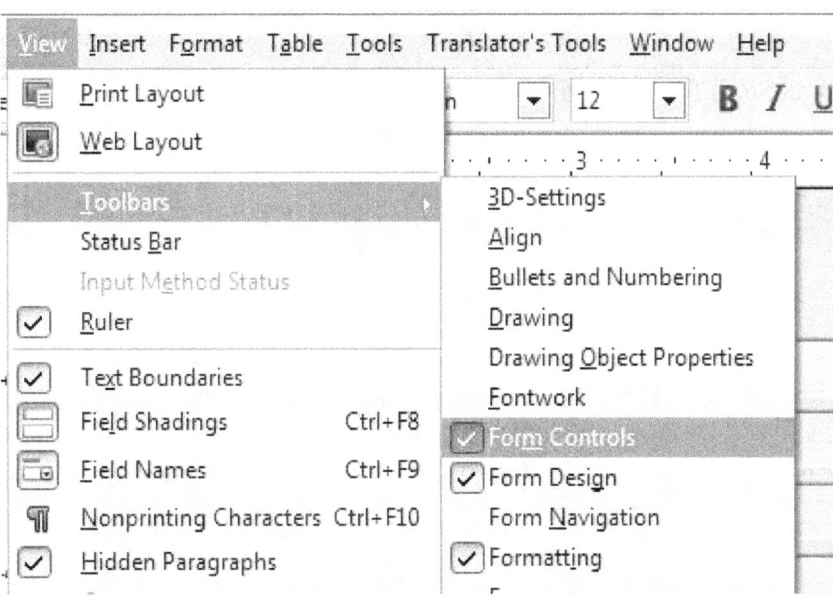

Figure 1

Figure 2

Step 4: Click the tool for the type of control that is desired.

Figure 3

Step 4: Click in the **Form Design** grid to position the control. Position the control by first placing the top left-hand corner in the desired location. Once the corner has been placed, hold and drag the other edge of the control field to the preferred location and then release the mouse button. The control will be inserted into the Form.

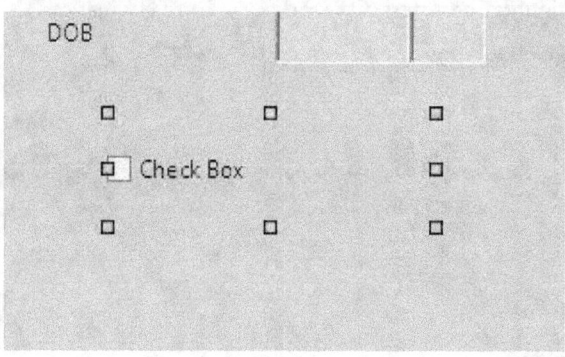

Figure 4

Step 5: Double-click on the new control. The **Properties** textbox will appear.

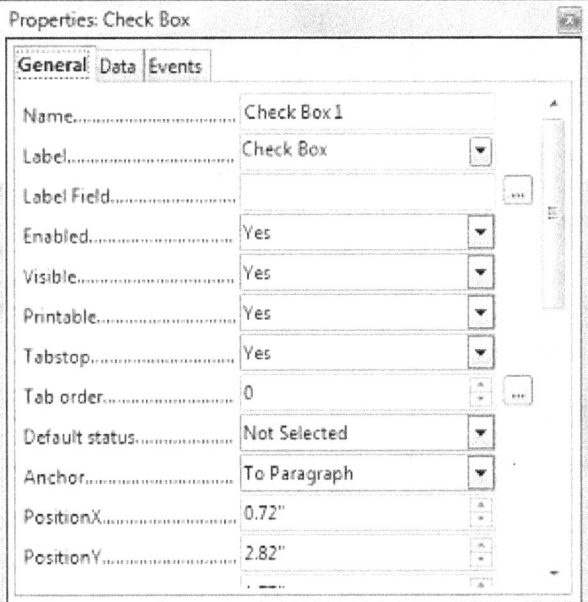

Figure 5

Step 6: Enter a name for the new control in the **Name** textbox. Enter the label that will be displayed next to the control in the **Label** textbox.

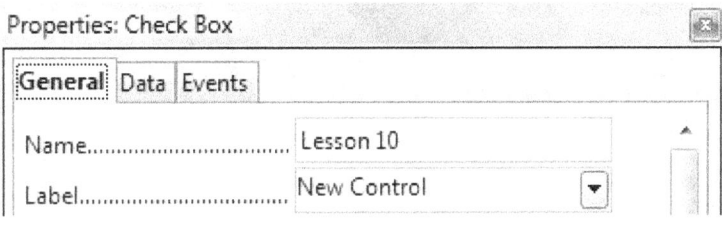

Figure 6

Step 7: Close the dialog box. The Label will be added to the new control.

Figure 7

Growth & Assessment

1. What is the most commonly used control?

2. What is clicked to position the control?

3. Checkboxes are another common control.

   a. TRUE

   b. FALSE

Section 2.11 – Adding Controls Using the Control Wizard

Section Objective:

- Learn how to add controls to a form using the Control Wizard.

The Control Wizard

The Control Wizard in OpenOffice Base helps users create controls for a form. Though there are many controls that can be created, the steps required to create each control are very similar; only minor variations are necessary depending on the type of control desired. The following steps outline how to access and use the **Control Wizard**.

Step 1: Open a form in Design View.

Step 2: Click **View**, located on the Menu Bar.

Step 3: From the **View** drop-down menu, scroll over **Toolbars** and select **Form Controls**. The **Form Controls** toolbar will appear vertically on the left-hand side of the screen.

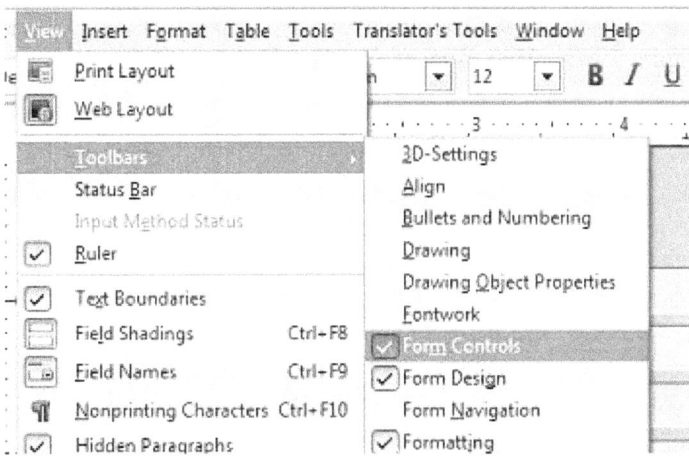

Figure 1

Figure 2

Step 4: Click the icon for the **List Box** or **Combo Box** control.

Figure 3

List Box – Displays a list of items users can choose from.

Combo Box – Allows users to select from a list of items while also allowing them to input items which are not listed.

Step 4: Click in the **Form Design** grid to position the control. Position the control by first placing the top left-hand corner in the desired location. Once the corner has been placed, hold and drag the other edge of the control field to the preferred location and then release the mouse button. The control will be inserted into the Form and the appropriate **Control Wizard** will open depending on which control was selected.

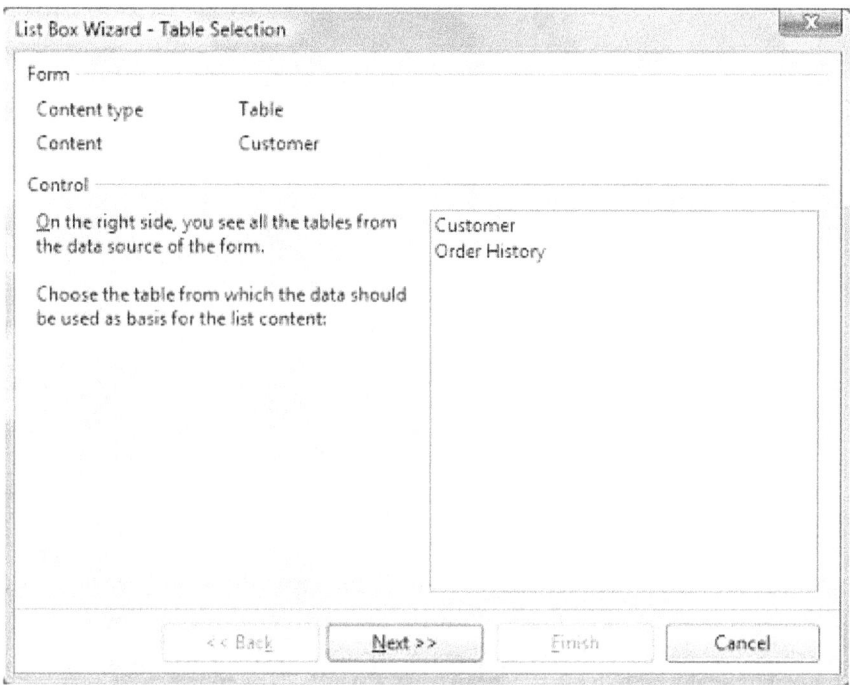

Figure 4

Step 5: Select a table or view that has been previously created to use as the foundation for the List or Combo Box. Once this has been done, click **Next** to continue.

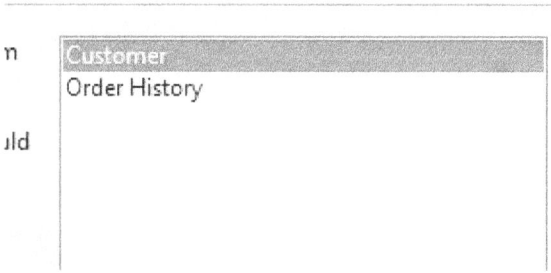

Figure 5

Step 6: Select the field(s) that contains the values that will be displayed in the list or combo box. Once this has been done, click **Next** to continue.

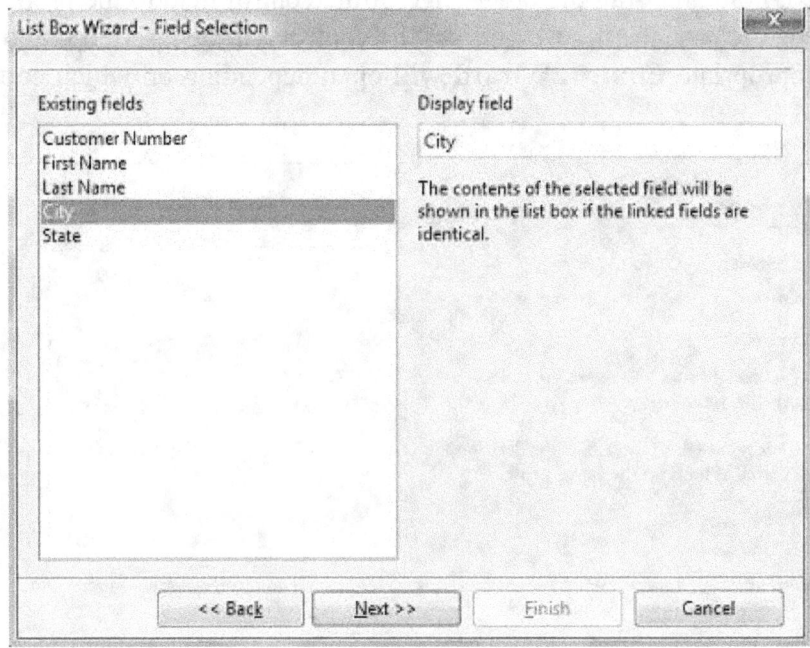

Figure 6

Step 7: It is at this step where the wizard will differ depending on the type of control that was inserted into the form. If a List box was selected, users will have the opportunity to tie what is in the field to what is displayed. A Combo Box however, will ask if the user wants fields saved only to the Form, or to both the Form and Table. Depending on the selected control, select the desired action.

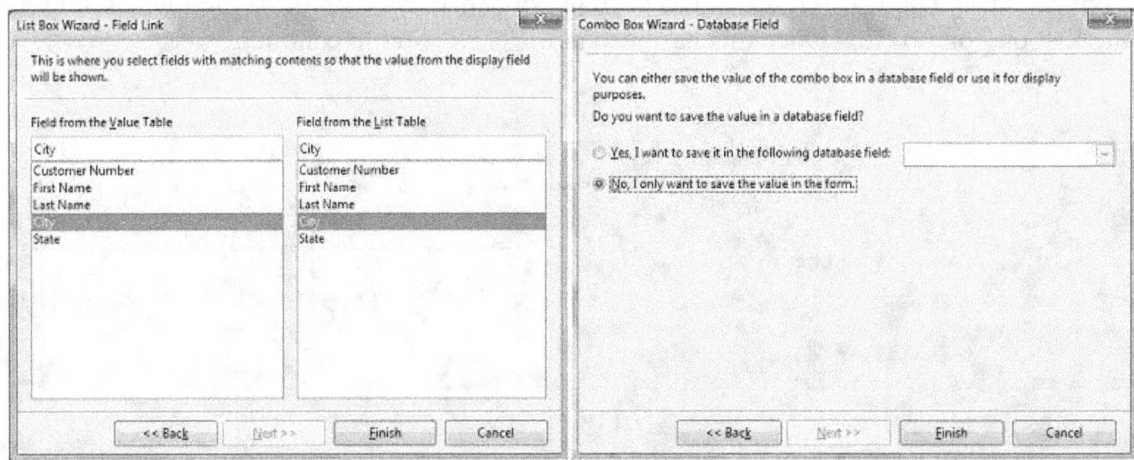

Figure 7

Step 8: Click **Finish** to exit the wizard and insert the control.

Figure 8

Growth & Assessment

1. The Control Wizard in OpenOffice Base helps the user create controls for a form.

    a. TRUE

    b. FALSE

2. What does a List Box do?

3. A Combo Box only displays a list of items the user can choose from.

    a. TRUE

    b. FALSE

Section 2.12 – Modifying the Layout of Fields on a Form

Section Objective:

- Learn to modify the layout of fields on a form.

Modifying the Layout of Fields

When creating a Form in OpenOffice Base, the application provides users with a few layout options regarding the fields' positions and sizes on the form. After creating the form, Base allows users to modify where the fields are located on the form, their size, and if they are to be displayed or not. This section explains how to move the fields to different locations on the form, how a field can be resized to fit the content, and how a field can be deleted if it is no longer needed.

Moving a Field

Step 1: Using the left mouse button, click a field on the form so it is highlighted with an outline.

Figure 1

Step 2: Click on the highlighted field and, while still holding the left mouse button, drag the field to the bottom of the form page. An outline of the field will appear as the cursor is moved. This outline shows where the field would be placed if the left mouse button was to be released.

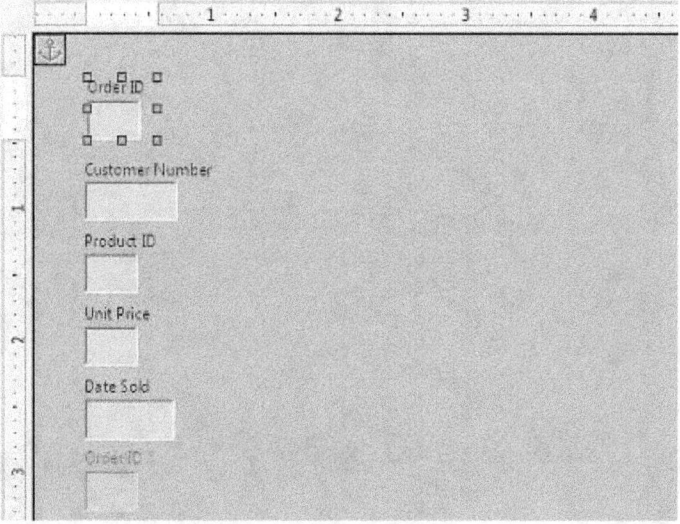

Figure 2

Step 3: Release the left mouse button, the field will be moved to the bottom of the form, as indicated by the outline.

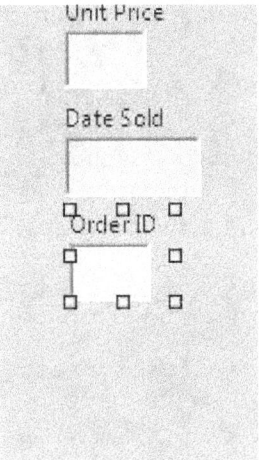

Figure 3

Changing the Size of a Field

Depending on what the user plans on entering into the form fields, the data may be too large to fit into the field textbox that Base provides. This is not a problem because the user has the ability to adjust the field textboxes to be any size needed. The next set of steps will outline how to quickly change the size of the Form fields.

Step 1: Select a field on the form so an outline, containing adjustment boxes, is visible around the field.

Step 2: Place the cursor on any of the adjustment boxes (the small squares in the outline), and then click and hold the left mouse button.

Figure 4

Step 3: Move the mouse to either shrink or enlarge the size of the Form field. Again, an outline of the field will appear as the cursor is moved to shows where the field would be placed if the left mouse button was released.

Step 4: Once the field outline has been changed to the desired width and height, release the left mouse button and the field will be changed to the specified size.

Figure 5

Removing a Field

Step 1: As with other modifications covered earlier in this section, select a field on the form so that there is an outline, containing adjustment boxes, visible around the field.

Step 2: Complete one of the three tasks given below to remove the field.

   a. Press the **Delete** button on the keyboard.

   b. Right-click on the field and then select **Cut**.

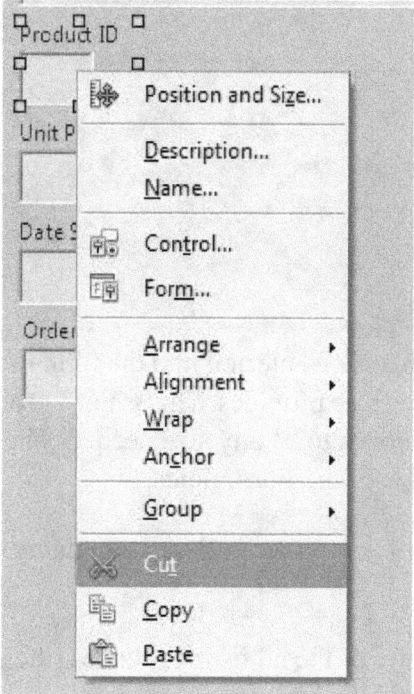

Figure 6

   c. Click **Edit**, located on the Menu Bar, and select **Cut** from the options available.

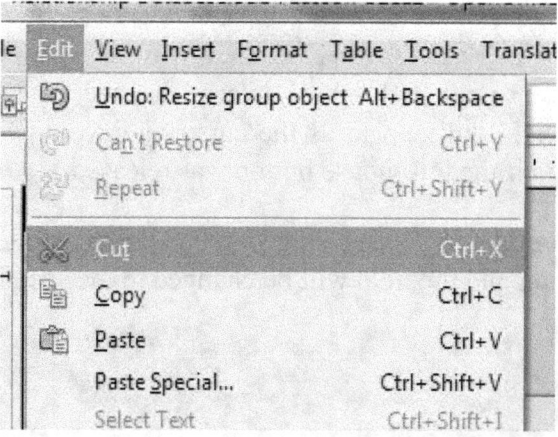

Figure 7

Note – Pressing the **Delete** key will permanently remove the field from the form. Using the two Cut options will remove the field to the **Clipboard**. The Cut field could be placed back into the Form using the **Paste** command.

Growth & Assessment

1. How many tasks are involved in removing a field?

2. When creating a Form in OpenOffice Base, the application provides the user with a few layout options regarding the fields' positions and sizes on the form.

    a. TRUE

    b. FALSE

3. What happens when a user presses the Delete key?

4. After creating the form, Base will not allow users to modify where the fields are located on the form, their size, or if they are to be displayed or not.

    a. TRUE

    b. FALSE

Section 2.13 – Creating a Relationship Between Tables

Section Objective:

- Learn how to create a relationship between tables.

Creating Table Relationships

In OpenOffice Base, one of the goals of a good database design is to remove data redundancy (duplicate data). To achieve this goal, users can divide data into many subject-based tables so that each fact (address, billing information, etc.) is represented only once. To do this, users must provide Base with the means by which to bring the divided information back together; this is done by placing common fields in tables that are related.

A good example of common fields in different tables would be if an online retailer, such as E-bay or Amazon, had one table named **Customer** and one named **Order History**. In both of these tables there would be a field named **Customer Number**. The two tables could then have a relationship added to them through that field. The following steps explain how something like this can be done but before beginning the steps below, create the following tables in a new Base database.

Customer

Customer Number	First Name	Last Name	City	State
1	Amy	Mitchell	Pittsburgh	PA
2	Bob	Salzer	Philadelphia	PA
3	Ryan	Dunn	Chester	PA
4	John	Davies	Bedford	PA

Figure 1

Order History

Order ID	Customer Number	Product ID	Unit Price	Date Sold
1	2	2312	25	05/05/11
2	2	1234	50	05/06/11
3	4	35341	1000	08/15/11
4	1	123123	11000	05/11/11

Figure 2

Now, follow the steps below to create a relationship between the two tables in OpenOffice Base.

Step 1: Click **Tools**, located on the Menu Bar.

Step 2: From the **Tools** drop-down menu, select **Relationships....** The **Relation Design** window will open with the **Add Tables** dialog box displayed.

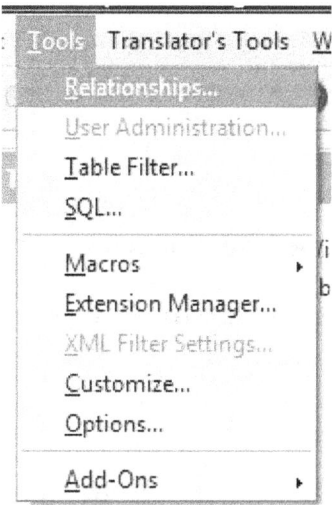

Figure 3

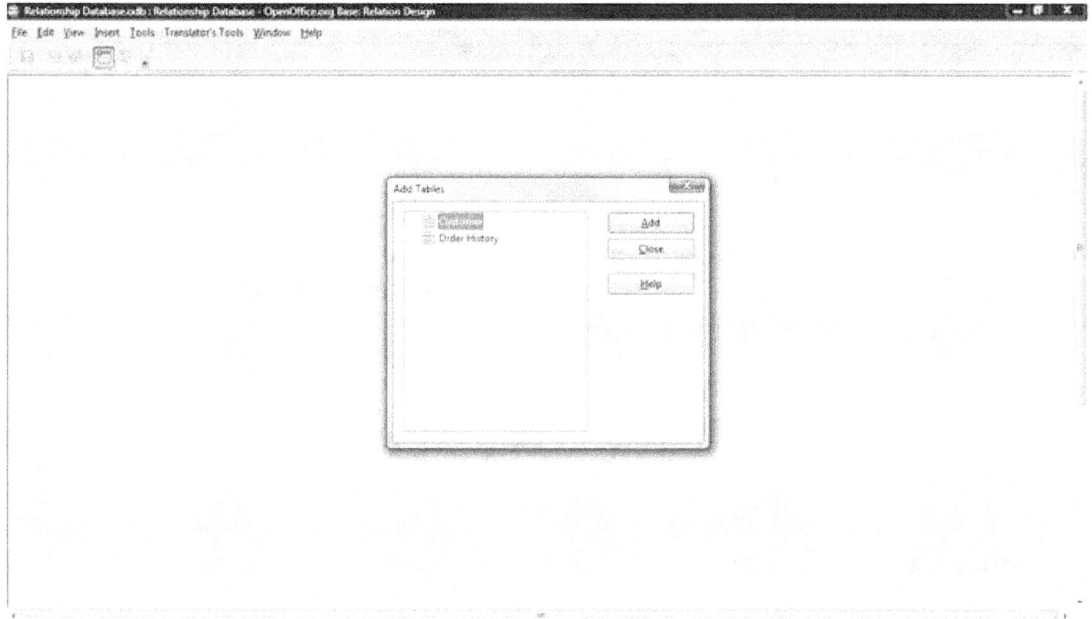

Figure 4

Step 3: Click on each table that will be a part of the relationship. This is done by clicking the **Add** button which will add them to the **Relation Design** window.

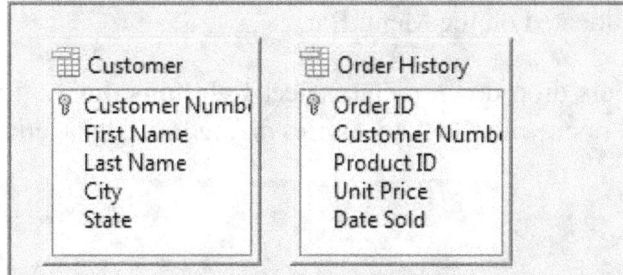

Figure 5

Step 4: Once the desired tables have been added to the Relation Design window, click the **Close** button located on the **Add Tables** dialog box. The dialog box will close.

Step 5: Click the **Customer Number** field in the **Customer** table, and then drag it to the top of the Customer Number field in the **Order History** table.

Step 6: Release the left mouse button. A line will be drawn connecting the two tables.

Figure 6

Step 7: Click the **Save** button on the Menu Bar and then close the **Relation Design** window. Now, there is a relationship between the **Customer** table and the **Order History** table through the **Customer Number** field.

Growth & Assessment

1. What is data redundancy?

2. To avoid redundancy users can divide data into many subject-based tables.

    a. TRUE

    b. FALSE

3. How are fields brought back together?

Section 2.14 – Adding a Subform Using the Form Wizard

Section Objective:

- Learn how to add a Subform by using the Form Wizard.

Creating a Subform

In OpenOffice Base, a **Subform** refers to a form within a form. It is used when a user wants to display data from multiple tables where a one-to-many relationship occurs. An example of this would be if a user wanted to display an order with the details of the order included. In this example, the main information of the order would be displayed on the form and the order details would be displayed in the **Subform**.

Before following the steps for adding a **Subform**, create a new database and two separate tables using the following data:

Customer:

Customer Number	First Name	Last Name	City	State
1	Amy	Mitchell	Pittsburgh	PA
2	Bob	Salzer	Philadelphia	PA
3	Ryan	Dunn	Chester	PA
4	John	Davies	Bedford	PA

Figure 1

Order History:

Order ID	Customer Number	Product ID	Unit Price	Date Sold
1	2	2312	25	05/05/11
2	2	1234	50	05/06/11
3	4	35341	1000	08/15/11
4	1	123123	11000	05/11/11

Figure 2

Step 1: Click on the **Forms** icon in the **Tasks** pane along the left-hand side of the application window.

Figure 3

Step 2: Double-click on **Use Wizard to Create Forms...** in the **Tasks** pane. The Form Wizard will open.

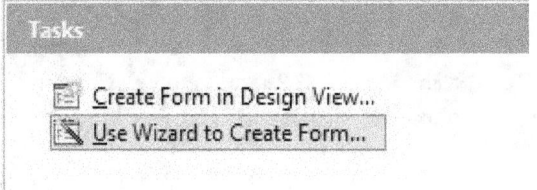

Figure 4

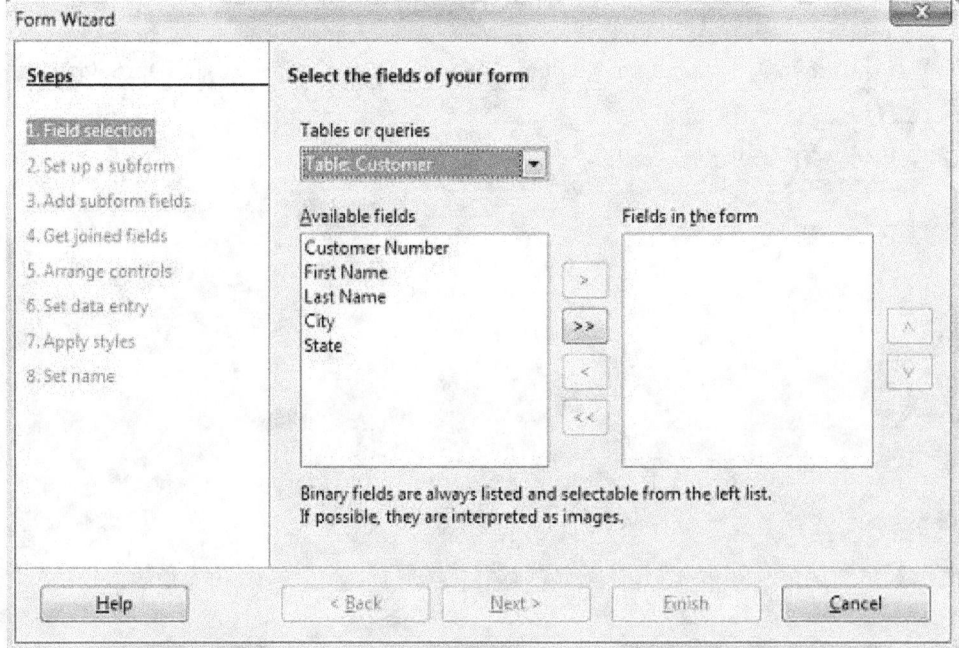

Figure 5

106

Step 3: On the first page of the wizard, **Field selection**, choose **Customer** and then use the **>>** button to move all of the fields into the **Fields in the Form** window. Once the desired fields have been moved to the **Fields in the Form** window, click the **Next** button to continue.

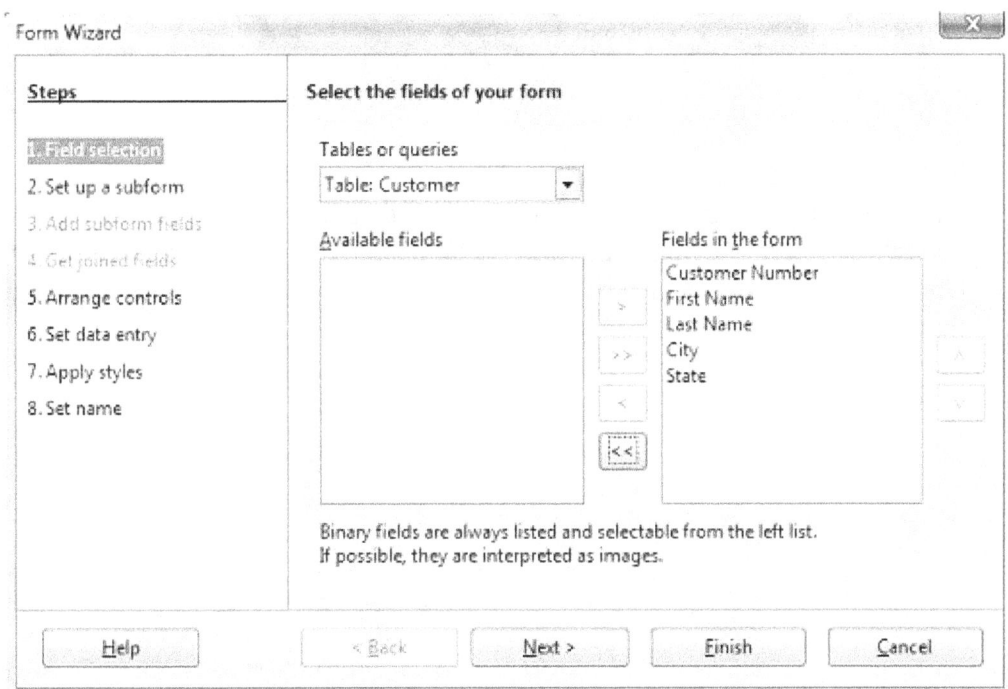

Figure 6

Step 4: On the second page of the wizard, **Set up a subform**, the user will begin to set up the Subform. Select the checkbox next to **Add Subform**. This will activate the rest of the options on the page.

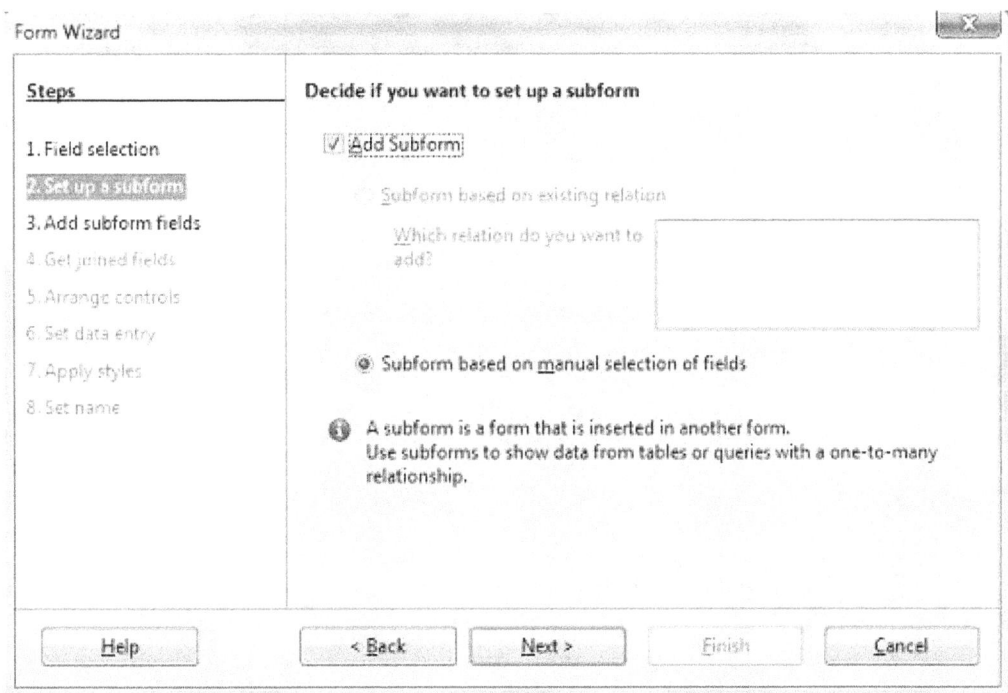

Figure 7

Step 5: Since table relationships haven't been created, the **Subform Based on Manual Selection of Fields** radio button is the only option and by default, is selected. Click the **Next** button to continue.

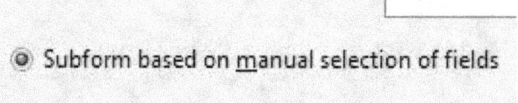

Figure 8

Step 6: The third page of the wizard, **Add subform fields**, is where users selects the table that will be used to pull fields from for the **Subform**. Select **Order History**, and click the **>>** button to move the desired fields to the **Fields in the Form** window. Once the desired fields have been moved to the **Fields in the Form** window, click the **Next** button to continue.

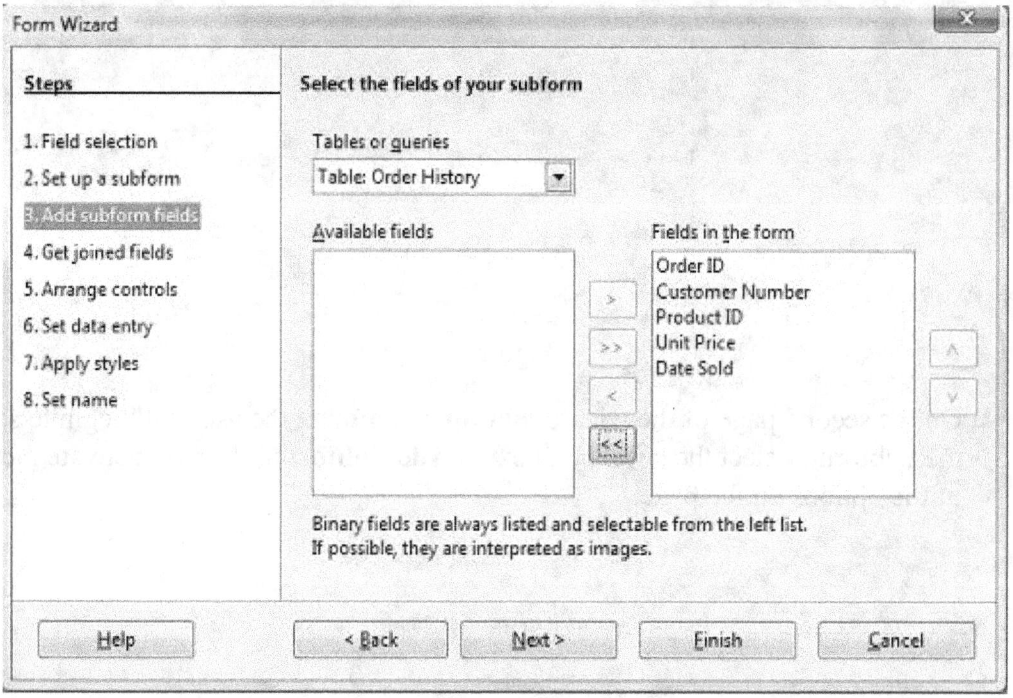

Figure 9

Step 7: The fourth page of the wizard, **Get joined fields**, is where users will specify which field in **Customer** has a relationship with a field in **Order History**. For this example, select **Customer Number** for both drop-down menus. Click the **Next** button to continue.

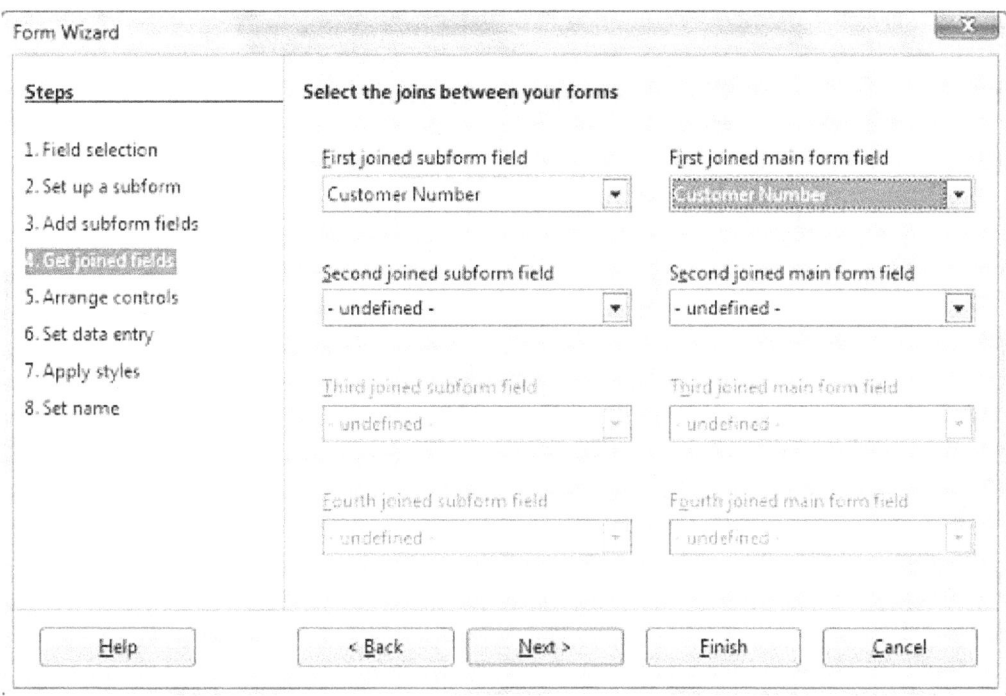

Figure 10

Step 8: The **Arrange controls** page is where users select the layout of both the **Form** and **Subform**. For this example choose the **Columnar – Labels Left** option for both **Form** and **Subform**.

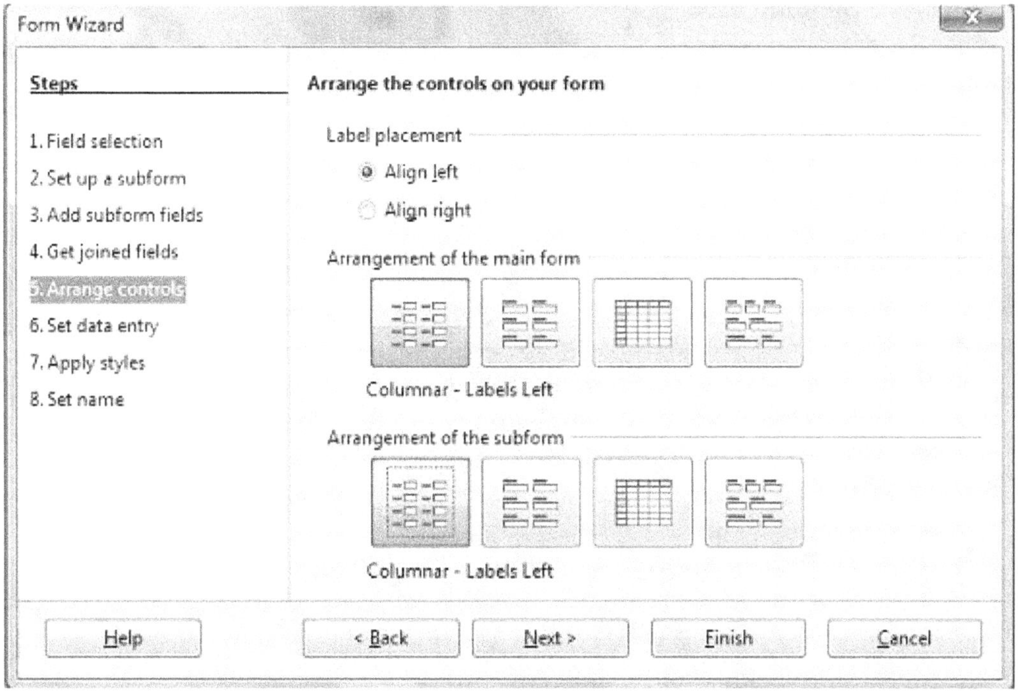

Figure 11

Step 9: Click **Finish** to close the Form Wizard and create a Form with a Subform.

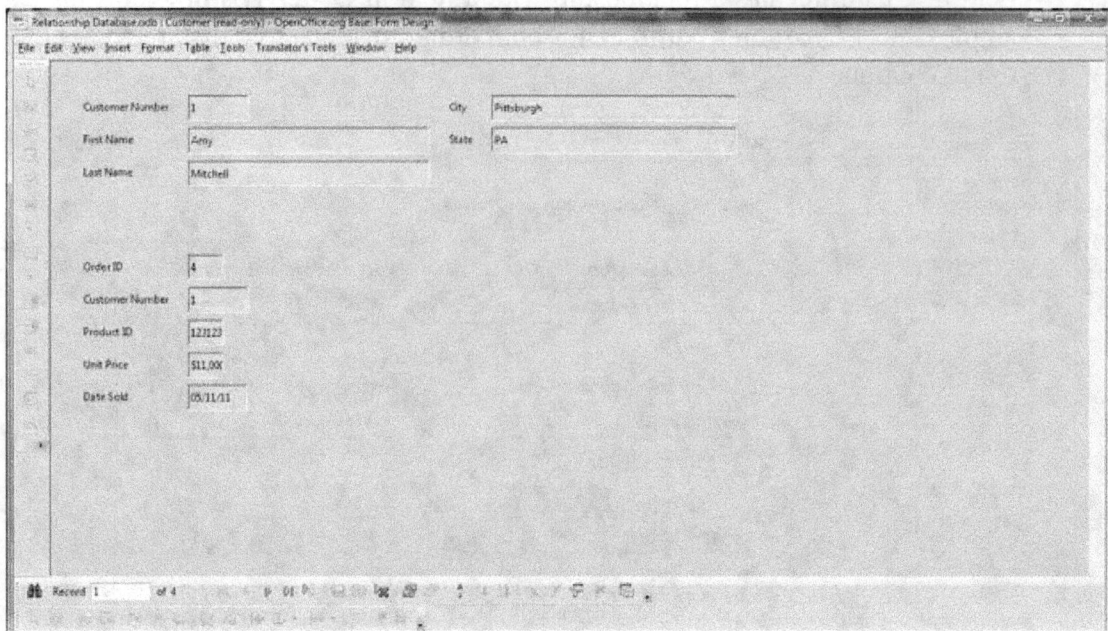

Figure 12

Growth & Assessment

1. What is the fourth page of the Form Wizard?

2. What is a Subform?

3. When is a Subform used?

Section 2.15 – Adding Symbols and Special Characters

Section Objective:

- Learn how to add symbols and special characters to tables and forms.

Adding Symbols and Special Characters

When adding data to a Base Table and/or Form, users may want to use a symbol or special character that does not appear on the keyboard. A large amount of symbols and special characters are available through the **Character** dialog box.

Use the **Character** dialog box to access symbols, characters from other languages, arrows, and other special characters. Users have the ability to format any characters entered into the application as if it were regular text, with the exception of the character's font, which is covered in the steps below.

Steps for adding Special Characters:

Step 1: Create a new Base Table or Form and place the insertion point in the record where the special character is needed.

Step 2: Right-click in the selected field to display the **Quick Menu**.

Figure 1

Step 3: From the Quick Menu, click **Special Character…**. The **Special Character** dialog box will open.

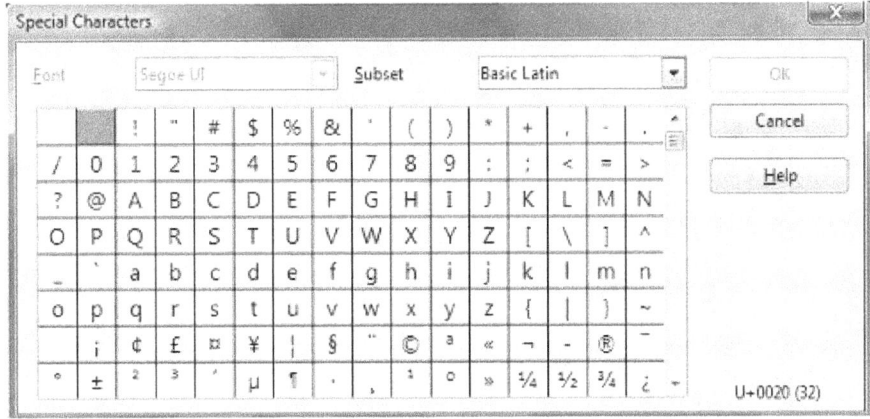

Figure 2

111

Step 4: The next portion of the Characters dialog box is the **Subset** drop-down list. The characters and symbols are broken down into subsets depending on what type they are. For example, sigma ($\sum$) is a Greek letter so it is placed under **Basic Greek**. Choose the desired character from the preferred subset.

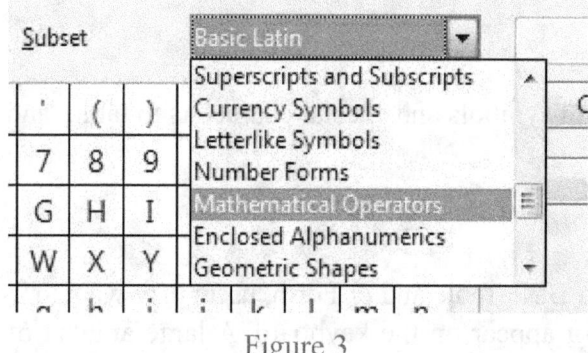

Figure 3

Step 5: Once the desired character has been selected, the character will be displayed in the bottom right-hand side of the screen. After verifying that it is the correct character, click **OK**. The selected character will appear in the Table/Form field.

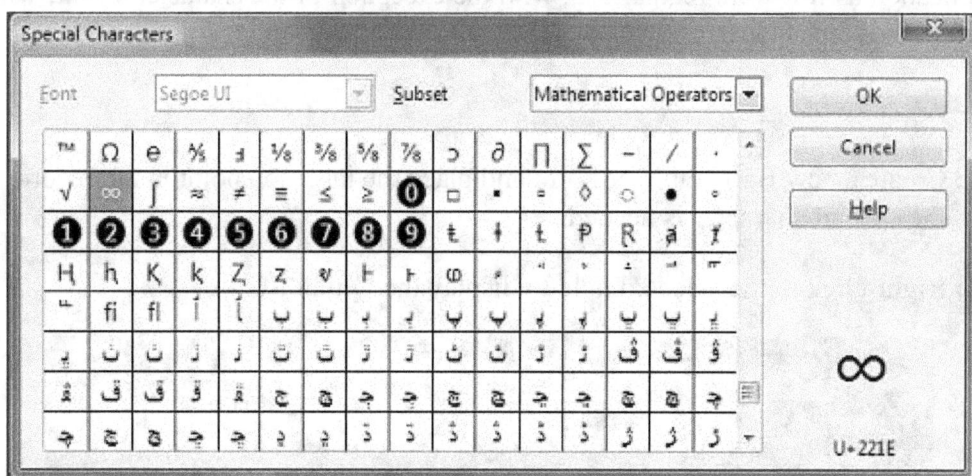

Figure 4

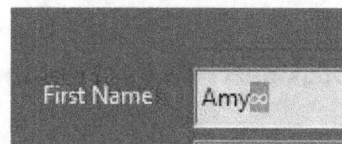

Figure 5

Growth & Assessment

1. What is the font used by the special characters?

2. Sigma would be found under Basic Latin subset.

    a. TRUE

    b. FALSE

3. Users can change the font of special characters.

    a. TRUE

    b. FALSE

4. Where are most of the symbols and special characters found?

Unit Three

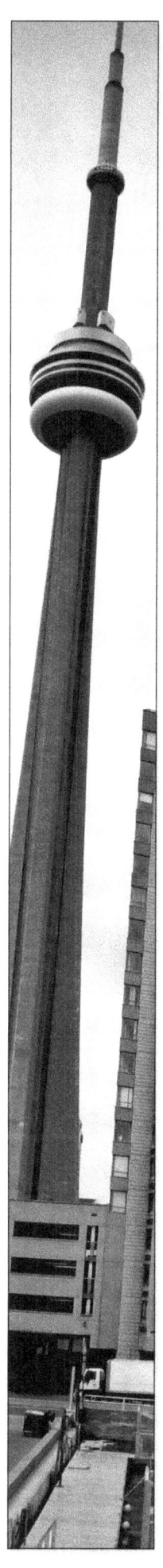

Section 3.1 – Sorting Information   116

Section 3.2 – Using the AutoFilter   119

Section 3.3 – Creating a Custom Filter   121

Section 3.4 – Moving Data Using Copy and Cut   124

Section 3.5 – Creating a Query in Design View   127

Section 3.6 – Creating a Query Using the Query Wizard   131

Section 3.7 – Using the Function Field   136

Section 3.8 – Restricting Data Using Field Type Settings   141

Section 3.9 – Restricting Data Using Field Length Settings   144

Section 3.10 – Creating a Report   146

Section 3.11 – Creating a Report Using the Report Wizard   149

Section 3.12 – Changing the Font, Size, and Color of the Text   156

Section 3.13 – Restricting Data Using the Combo Box   160

Section 3.14 – Updating Information within a Table   165

Section 3.15 – Deleting Information within a Table   167

Section 3.1 – Sorting Information

Section Objective:

- Learn how to sort information.

Sorting Information

OpenOffice Base allows users to sort a field to better organize the information. The user can sort the information in an Ascending or Descending order, or create a multi-level sort; to meet a variety of specifications. The following steps outline how both of these sorting options are done in OpenOffice Base.

Sorting in an Ascending or Descending Order

Step 1: Select the column(s) that will be sorted.

Step 2: From the **Formatting Toolbar**, click either the **Ascending** or **Descending** buttons to sort the data. Once the desired option has been selected, the data will be sorted.

Figure 1

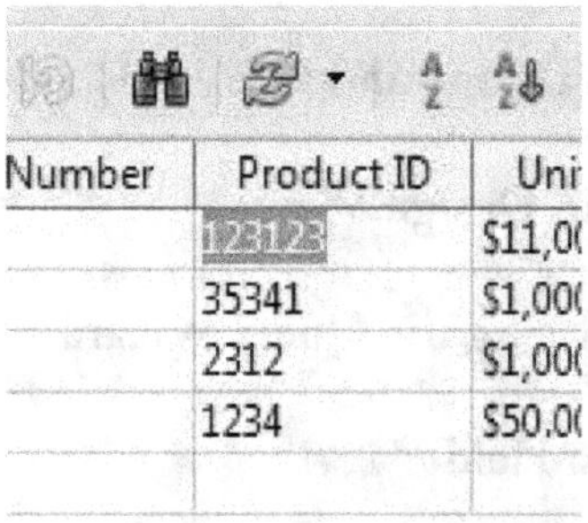

Figure 2

Note – When sorting in Base using the toolbar, the value in the selected cell is treated as a heading and will not be sorted with the rest of the list.

Creating Multi-level Sorts

Step 1: Select a cell in the desired column.

Step 2: Click the **Sort** button on the **Toolbar**. The **Sort** dialog box will appear.

Figure 3

Step 3: In the **Sort By** drop-down menu, select which column(s) the sort will be applied to.

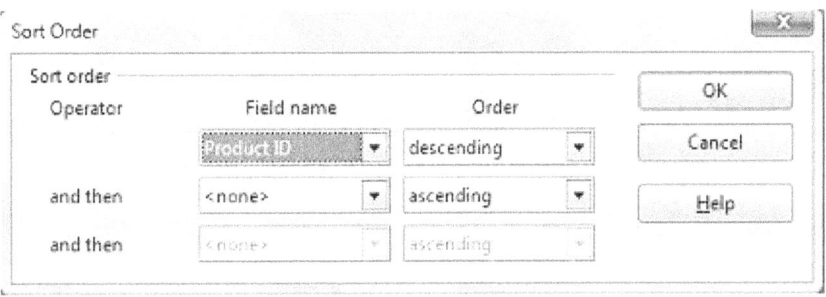

Figure 4

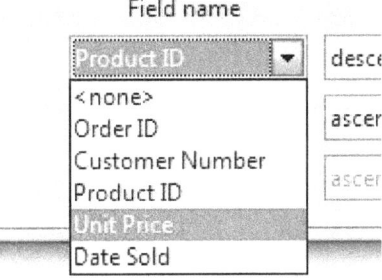

Figure 5

Step 4: On the right side of the **Sort By** drop-down menu, select whether the data should be sorted in an **Ascending** or **Descending** order.

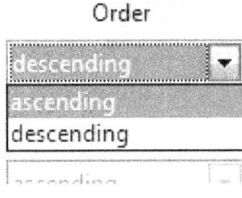

Figure 6

Step 5: In the **Then By** drop-down menu, choose a secondary column to sort by; meaning, if there are duplicate values in column 1, the user can set secondary criteria.

Step 6: Click **OK**. The data will be sorted based on the options selected.

Growth & Assessment

1. Users can sort information in an Ascending or Descending order.

    a. TRUE

    b. FALSE

2. What other type of sort can be created besides Ascending and Descending?

3. When sorting in Base using the toolbar, the value in the selected cell is treated as a heading and will not be sorted with the rest of the list.

    a. TRUE

    b. FALSE

Section 3.2 – Using the AutoFilter

Section Objective:

- Learn how to limit the data that appears on the screen by using an AutoFilter.

The AutoFilter

In OpenOffice Base, using **Filters** allows users to limit the rows and columns that are displayed in the table. For example, if a user created a table that listed every sale made by a company, but only wanted to view the number of sales for widgets, then the user would set a filter to show only the rows that were widget sales. Base allows users to create **AutoFilters**, which are generic filters that can be used on any type of data, for each column of the table. When accessed, they display column-specific pull-down menus from which the user can set up a filter. The following steps outline how to create an AutoFilter in OpenOffice Base.

Step 1: Create a new table in Base and enter the data shown in the figure below.

Employee ID	First Name	Last Name	District	# of Clients	Sales Amount
1	John	Davies	Philadelphia	9	1235241.00
2	Ken	Paul	Philadelphia	7	1234234.00
3	Amy	Hoch	Pittsburgh	16	8342412.00
4	Chris	Mitchell	Pittsburgh	12	12312312.00
5	Josh	Flaim	Pittsburgh	14	7463134.00
6	John	Riggins	Los Angeles	11	5832953.00
7	Amy	Krallinger	Los Angeles	6	981573.00

Figure 1

Step 2: Select either of the cells in the **First Name** column that contains the text "**John**."

Step 3: Click the **AutoFilter** button, located on the **Toolbar**. Base will automatically filter the table so that only records with the **Department** equal to **ID** are shown.

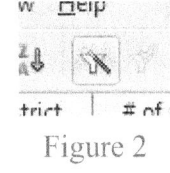

Figure 2

Employee ID	First Name	Last Name	District	# of Clients	Sales Amount
1	John	Davies	Philadelphia	9	1235241.00
6	John	Riggins	Los Angeles	11	5832953.00

Figure 3

Step 4: Click on the **Apply Filter** button on the Toolbar. This will temporarily remove the filter from the table. Base will still save the Filter criteria so if the user were to click the Apply Filter button a second time, the filter would be re-applied.

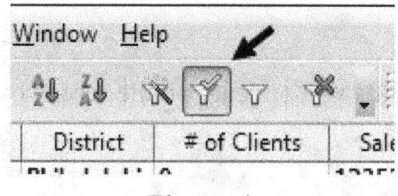

Figure 4

Step 5: Click the **Remove Filter/Sort** button, located on the Toolbar. This will remove the filter from the table and also delete the criteria from the AutoFilter's memory.

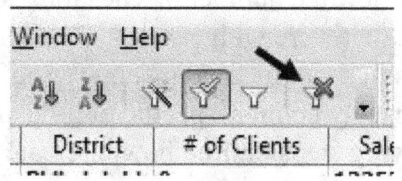

Figure 5

Growth & Assessment

1. What is an AutoFilter?

2. In OpenOffice Base, using Filters allows users to limit the rows and columns that are displayed in the table.

    a. TRUE

    b. FALSE

3. What happens when an AutoFilter is accessed?

4. Why would a filter be used?

Section 3.3 – Creating a Custom Filter

Section Objective:

- Learn how to create a custom filter.

Creating a Custom Filter

OpenOffice Base allows users to create a Custom Filter and apply it to a table, form, or query to filter the data based on specifications by the user. This is useful when trying to filter a table containing a large amount of data because by specifying the type of data needed, Base automatically filters the table for the data. The following steps explain how a Custom Filter can be created and applied to a Table in OpenOffice Base.

Note – Before following the steps, create a table containing the same data as the table show in the figure below.

	Employee ID	First Name	Last Name	District	# of Clients	Sales Amount
▷	1	John	Davies	Philadelphia	9	1235241.00
	2	Ken	Paul	Philadelphia	7	1234234.00
	3	Amy	Hoch	Pittsburgh	16	8342412.00
	4	Chris	Mitchell	Pittsburgh	12	12312312.00
	5	Josh	Flaim	Pittsburgh	14	7463134.00
	6	John	Riggins	Los Angeles	11	5832953.00
	7	Amy	Krallinger	Los Angeles	6	981573.00

Figure 1

Step 1: Click anywhere in the column or control that corresponds to the first field that will be filtered.

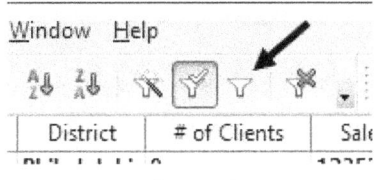

Figure 2

Step 2: Click the **Standard Filter** button, located on the **Toolbar**. The **Standard Filter** dialog box will appear.

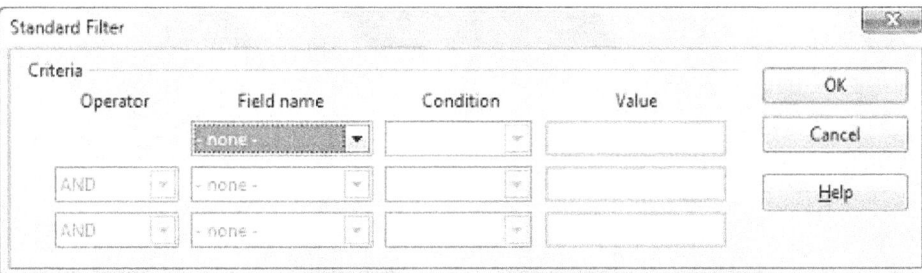

Figure 3

121

Step 3: In the **Field Name** pull-down list, select the first field the data will be filtered by. For this example choose **First Name**.

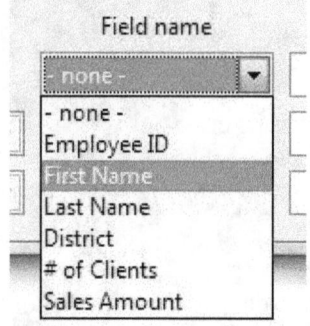

Figure 4

Step 4: In the **Condition** pull-down list, select the operator the data will be filtered by. For this example choose "**=**."

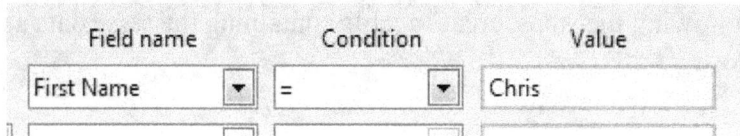

Figure 5

Step 5: In the **Value** pull-down list, select which value the data will be filtered by. For this example choose "**Chris**."

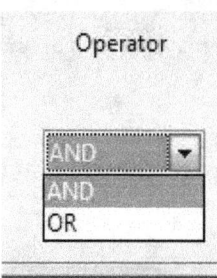

Figure 6

Step 6: To add a second criteria to the filter, select a value in the **Operator** pull-down list. For this example select the **And** value. This means that both criteria must be met for the value to be shown in the database.

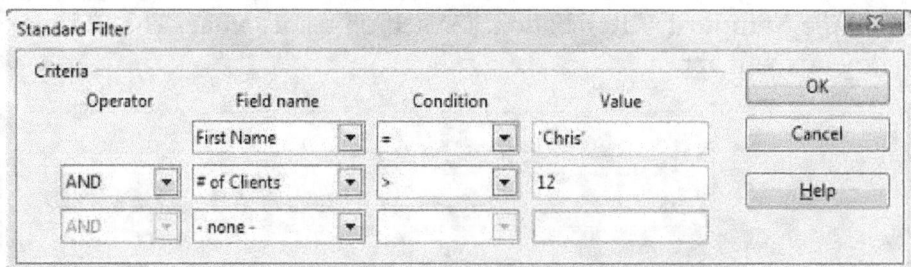

Figure 7

Note – If **Or** was selected, any data that was a match to one or more selected criteria would be displayed in the database.

Step 7: In the **Field** drop-down box, choose **Items Sold**; in the **Condition** drop-down box, select **>** and in the **Value** textbox, type **12**.

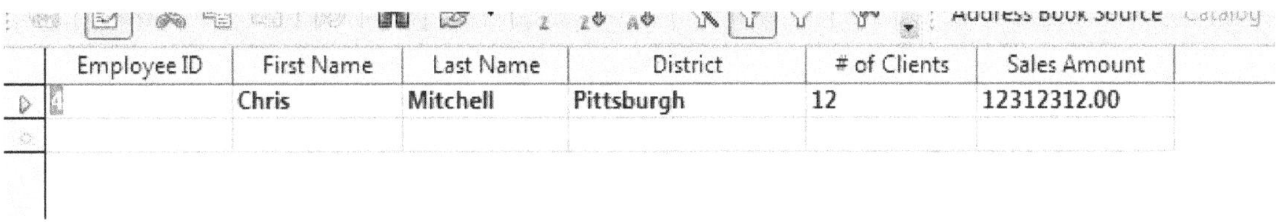

Employee ID	First Name	Last Name	District	# of Clients	Sales Amount
4	Chris	Mitchell	Pittsburgh	12	12312312.00

Figure 8

Step 8: Click **Ok**. The filter will be added to the database table.

Growth & Assessment

1. OpenOffice Base allows users to create a Custom Filter.

    a. TRUE

    b. FALSE

2. What happens if Or is selected in the Operator pull-down list?

3. When is a Custom Filter useful?

4. Where is the Standard Filter button located?

Section 3.4 – Moving Data Using Copy and Cut

Section Objective:

- Learn how to move data in a Base table using Copy and Cut.

Moving Data Using Copy and Cut

Working with data in an OpenOffice Base table can be time consuming. If a user has a large group of data that needs to be copied or moved from one table to another, manually reentering the data is ineffective. Base provides an alternative method, the **Cut** and **Copy** techniques. By using these techniques, users can quickly move and copy data to another table.

This section outlines how users can use the Cut and Copy techniques to effectively move data from one table to another in a database. Before following the steps, create a table containing the data shown in the figure below.

Order ID	Customer Number	Product ID	Unit Price	Date Sold
2	2	1234	$50.00	05/06/11
3	4	35341	$1,000.00	08/15/11
4	1	123123	$11,000.00	05/11/11
1	2	2312	$25.00	05/05/11

Figure 1

The Cut Technique

The following steps explain the Cut technique. Cutting moves the data from one table cell to a different cell, while deleting the data from the original cell.

Step 1: Open up the table in **Data View**. Select the first cell in the "**Product ID**" field.

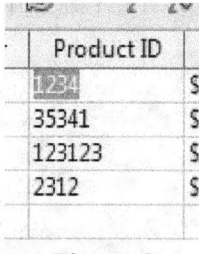

Figure 2

Step 2: Click **Edit**, located on the Menu Bar.

Step 3: From the **Edit** drop-down menu, click **Cut**. The text will be removed from the selected cell.

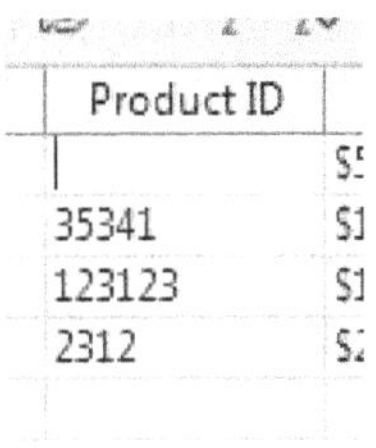

Figure 3

Note – The keyboard shortcut **CTRL + X** will also cut the data.

Step 4: Select the cell under the "**Product ID**" field for the second record.

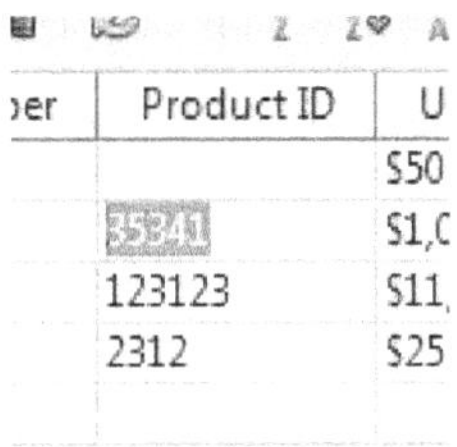

Figure 4

Step 5: Once again, click **Edit** on the Menu Bar.

Step 6: From the Edit drop-down menu, select **Paste**. The information will be inserted into the new cell.

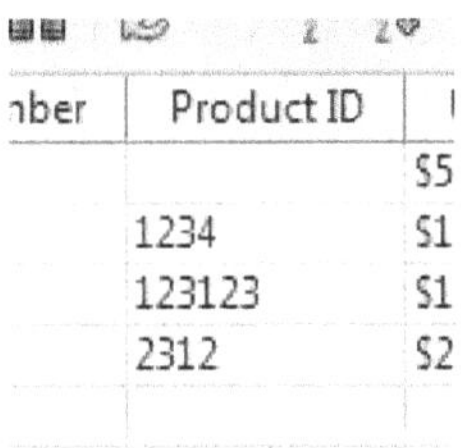

Figure 5

Note – The keyboard shortcut **CTRL + V** will also paste the data.

The Copy Technique

Copy and Paste works well for duplicating formulas, values, and labels without reentering them. When users Copy information, the information remains in the original location.

Step 1: Select the cell under **Product ID** field for the third record in the table.

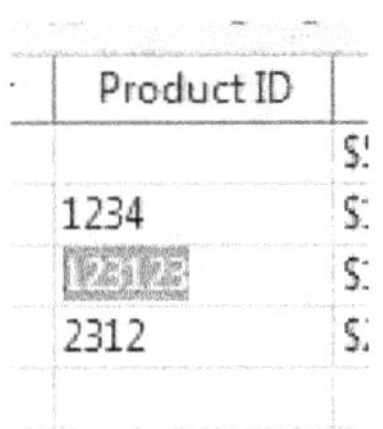

Figure 6

Step 2: From the **Edit** drop-down menu, click **Copy**. The text will remain in the selected cell.

    Note – The keyboard shortcut **CTRL + C** will also copy the data.

Step 3: Select the cell in the **Product ID** field for the first record.

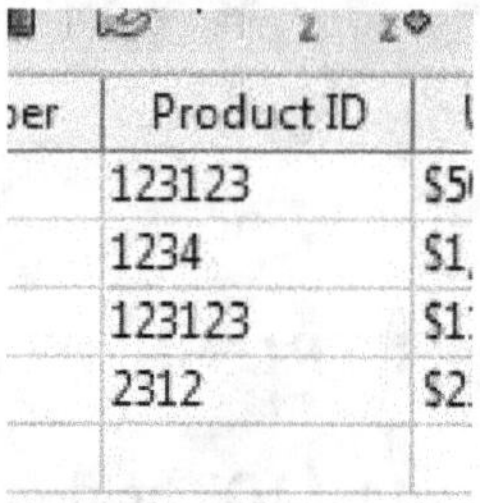

Figure 7

Step 4: From the **Edit** drop-down menu, click **Paste**. The information will be inserted into the new cell and also remain in the original cell.

Growth & Assessment

1. What is the keyboard shortcut for Cut?

2. Working with data in Base is normally a quick process.

    a. TRUE

    b. FALSE

3. What two features in Base allow users to quickly copy or move a large group of data from one table to another?

4. What is the keyboard shortcut for Paste?

Section 3.5 – Creating a Query in Design View

Section Objective:

- Learn how to create a query in Design view.

Creating Queries

In OpenOffice Base, **Queries** are a way to ask questions about the data. The application saves each query in the database as if it were any other database object. Once the query has been saved, users can run it at any time to look at the live data that meets the specified criteria. The following steps outline how to create a query in Design view.

Step 1: Create a new database and create a table that has the same information shown in the figure below. Name the table "**Query Table**."

	Employee ID	First Name	Last Name	District	# of Clients	Sales Amount
▷	1	John	Davies	Philadelphia	9	1235241.00
	2	Ken	Paul	Philadelphia	7	1234234.00
	3	Amy	Hoch	Pittsburgh	16	8342412.00
	4	Chris	Mitchell	Pittsburgh	12	12312312.00
	5	Josh	Flaim	Pittsburgh	14	7463134.00
	6	John	Riggins	Los Angeles	11	5832953.00
	7	Amy	Krallinger	Los Angeles	6	981573.00

Figure 1

Step 2: In the database pane click **Queries**.

Figure 2

127

Step 3: In the **Tasks** pane, double-click on **Create Query in Design View…**. The **Query Design** window will open.

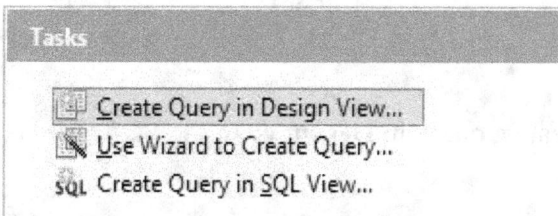

Figure 3

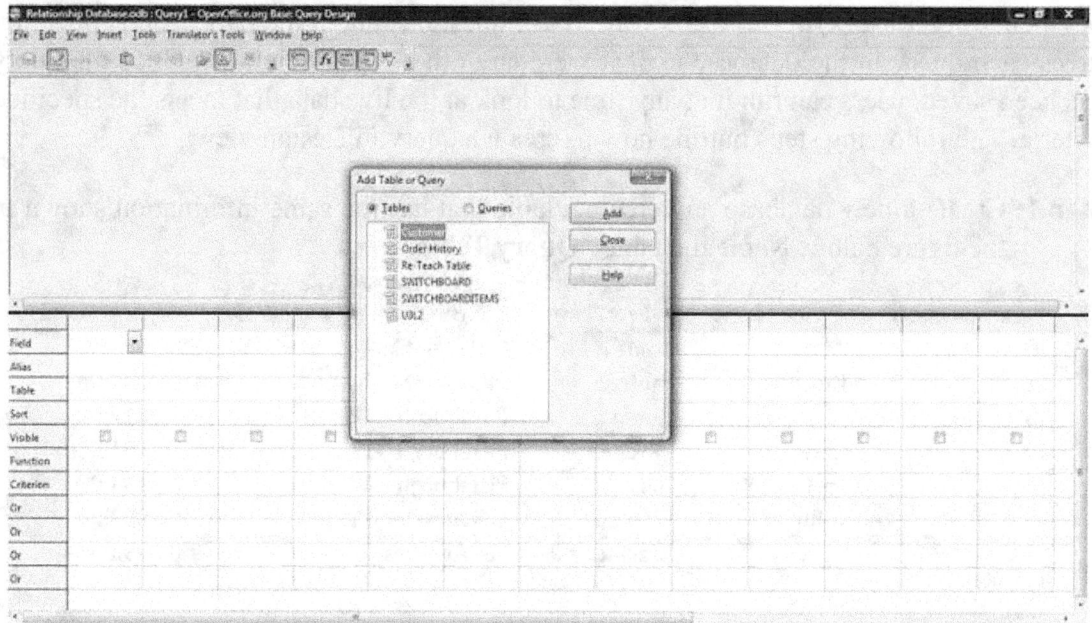

Figure 4

Step 4: The **Add Table or Query** dialog box will automatically open along with the Query Design window. Select the radio button next to **Tables**.

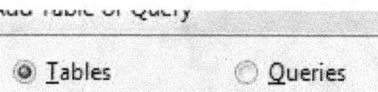

Figure 5

Step 5: Select the tables that will be added to the query by clicking **Add**. Once a table has been added to the query, the table will be displayed in the Query Design window.

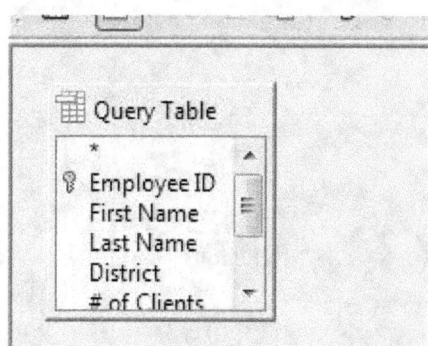

Figure 6

Step 6: Once all of the desired tables have been added to the query, click **Close**. The **Add Table or Query** dialog box will close leaving only the Query Design window.

Step 7: Double-click the fields that will be added to the query. As the fields are selected, Base will add them to the Field List at the bottom of the screen.

Field	First Name ▼	Last Name	District	
Alias				
Table	Query Table	Query Table	Query Table	
Sort				
Visible	✓	✓	✓	☐
Function				

Figure 7

Note – Double-click the **asterisk** to include all the columns from a particular table.

Step 8: Arrange the fields from left to right based on the preferred order in which they will appear in the **Query Results**.

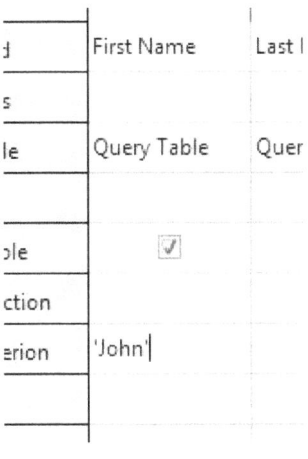

Figure 8

Step 9: Place any desired Filters to limit the data shown in the **Criterion** box.

Table	Query Table	Query 1
Sort	(not sorted) ▼	
Visible	(not sorted) / ascending / descending	
Function		
Criterion	'John'	
Or		

Figure 9

Note – Users have the ability to add a separate filter expression to each field.

Step 10: Use the **Sort** box in the **Field List** to select the preferred way in which the fields will be sorted.

Figure 10

Step 11: Within the Toolbar, click the **Run Query** button. The results of the query will be presented in a database.

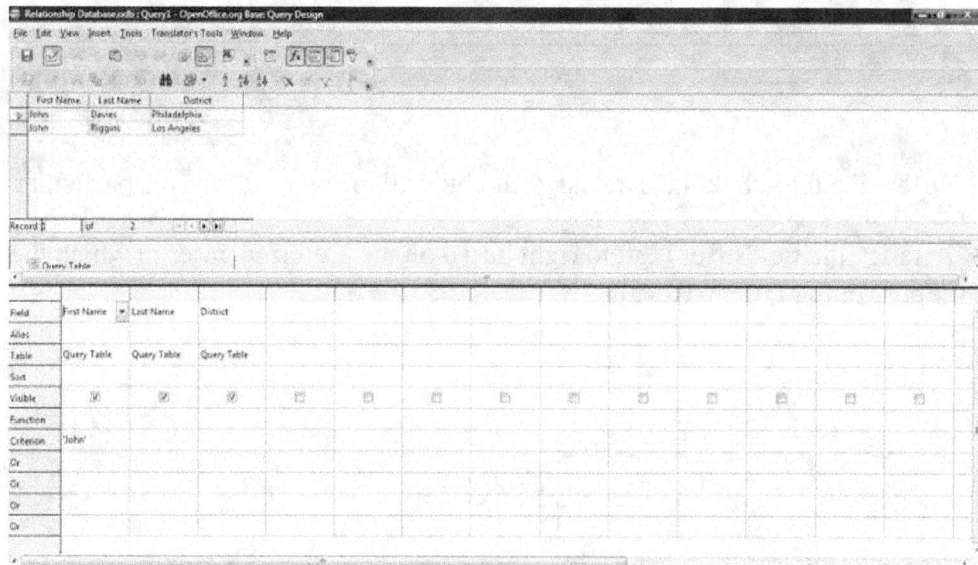

Figure 11

Growth & Assessment

1. What happens when the asterisk is double-clicked in the Query Results?

2. Once the query has been saved, the user can run it at any time to look at the live data that meets the specified criteria.

   a. TRUE

   b. FALSE

3. Users are unable to add a separate filter expression to each field.

   a. TRUE

   b. FALSE

4. What are queries used for?

Section 3.6 – Creating a Query Using the Query Wizard

Section Objective:

- Learn how to create a query with the Query Wizard.

The Query Wizard

In OpenOffice Base, the **Query Wizard** works by asking the user a series of questions, and then creating a query that fits the answers that were provided. The following steps outline how a user can use the Query Wizard to create queries for a database.

Step 1: Create a new database and create a table that has the same information shown in the figure below. Name the table **Query Wizard Table**.

Employee ID	First Name	Last Name	District	# of Clients	Sales Amount
1	John	Davies	Philadelphia	9	1235241.00
2	Ken	Paul	Philadelphia	7	1234234.00
3	Amy	Hoch	Pittsburgh	16	8342412.00
4	Chris	Mitchell	Pittsburgh	12	12312312.00
5	Josh	Flaim	Pittsburgh	14	7463134.00
6	John	Riggins	Los Angeles	11	5832953.00
7	Amy	Krallinger	Los Angeles	6	981573.00

Figure 1

Step 2: In the database pane, click **Queries**.

Figure 2

Step 3: In the **Tasks** pane, double-click on **Use wizard to Create Query…**. The **Query Wizard** dialog box will appear.

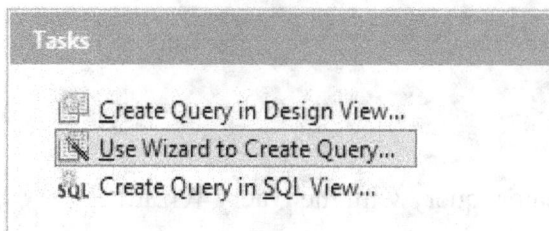

Figure 3

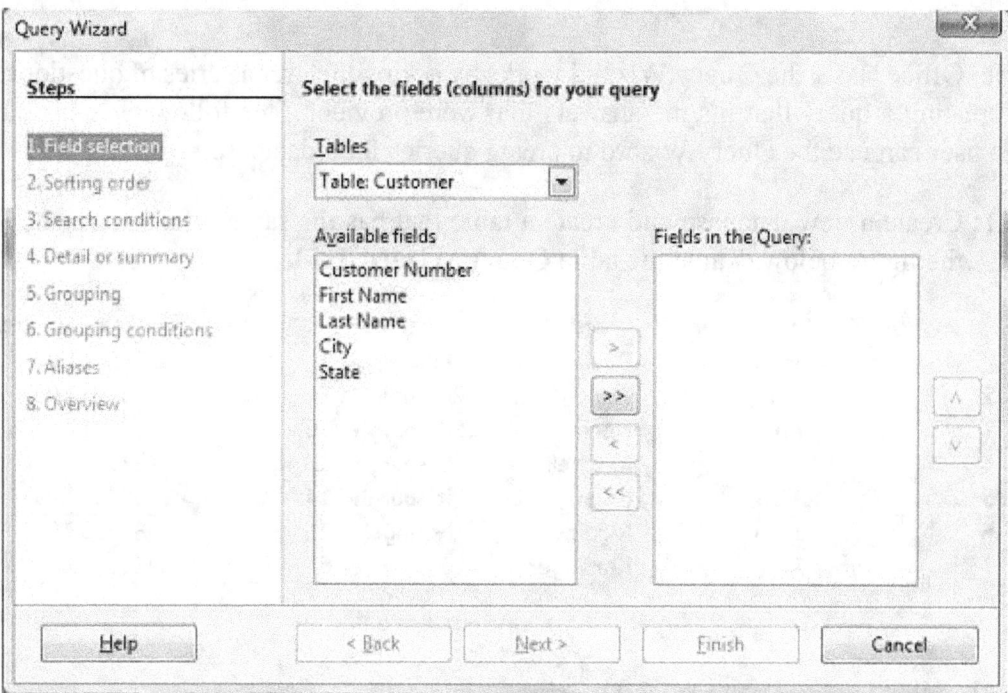

Figure 4

Step 4: The first screen of the wizard is the **Field Selection** screen. In this screen users have the ability to select the table which the fields will be pulled from, and then move those fields to be included in the query. This is done by moving the desired fields from the **Available Fields** window to the **Fields in the Query** window. For the purpose of this example, move all of the fields in the **Available Fields** window to the **Fields in the Query** window. Once all of the fields have been moved, click **Next** to move to the next screen.

Figure 5

Step 5: The **Sorting Order** screen is the next step in the wizard. From this screen, users have the ability to sort the query by any of the fields previously selected. Users also have the ability to sort in an **Ascending** or **Descending** order. For this example, sort by the **First Name** field in **Ascending** order. Once this has been done, click **Next** to move to the next screen.

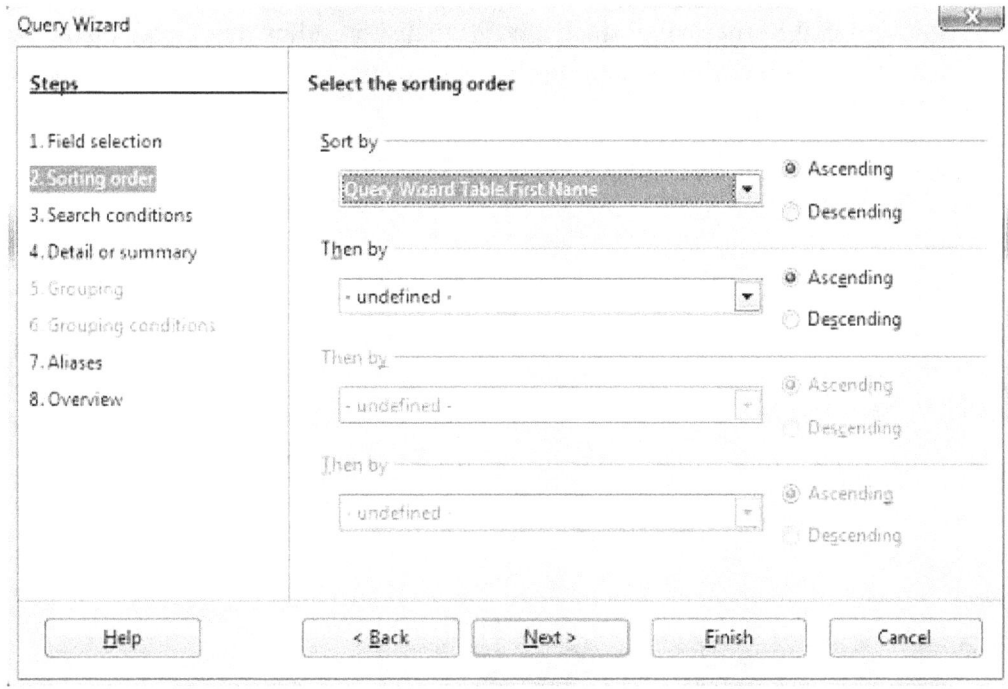

Figure 6

133

Step 6: The next screen of the wizard is the **Search Conditions** screen. Here, users have the ability to decide which records will be displayed, and which records will be filtered out. In the **Fields** drop-down menu, select the fields to include in the query on the **Fields Selection** page. Use the three drop-down menus to specify which records will be shown when the query is run. For this example, search for people with a first name equal to "**Bill**."

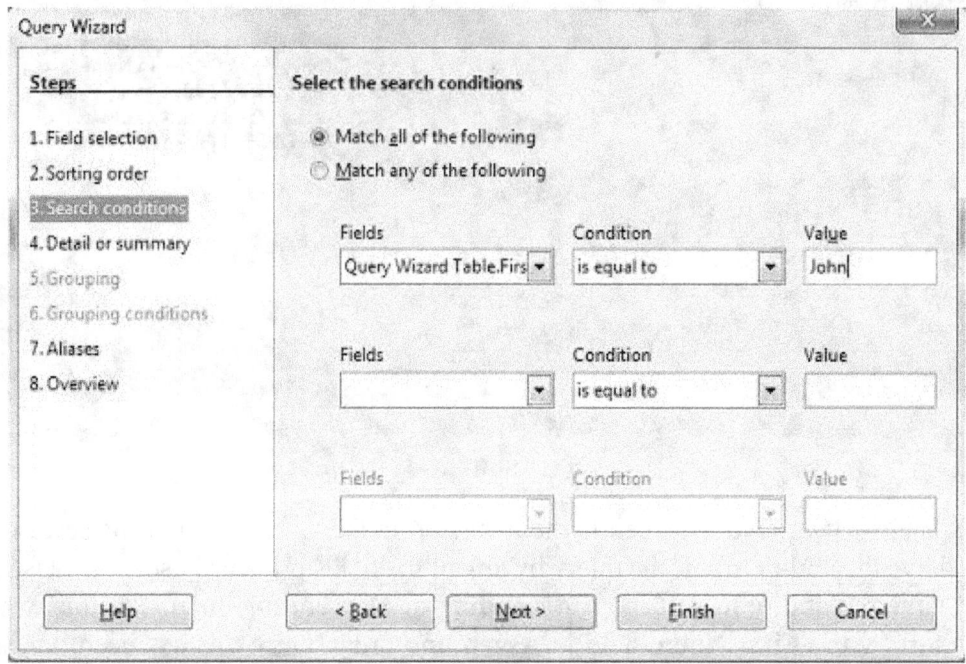

Figure 7

Step 7: After setting the criteria for which records to display, click the 8th step on the wizard to display the **Overview** page. On this page, type "**Wizard Query**" in the **Name of the Query** textbox.

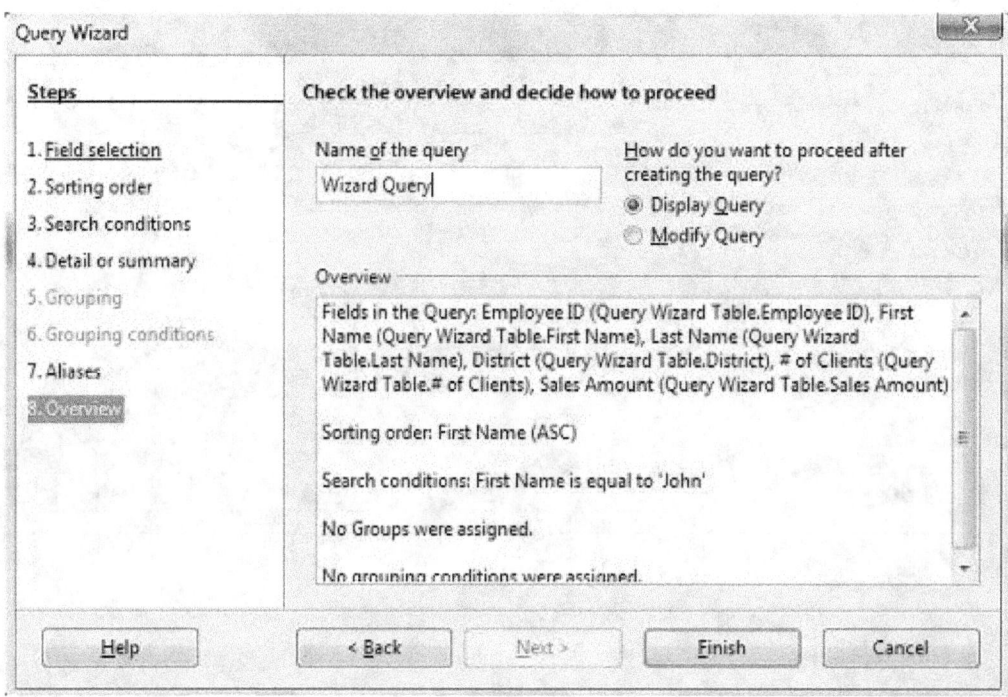

Figure 8

Step 8: After naming the query, enough information has been entered for the query to run. Click the **Finish** button and Base will automatically run the query and provide the results in the **Data View** window.

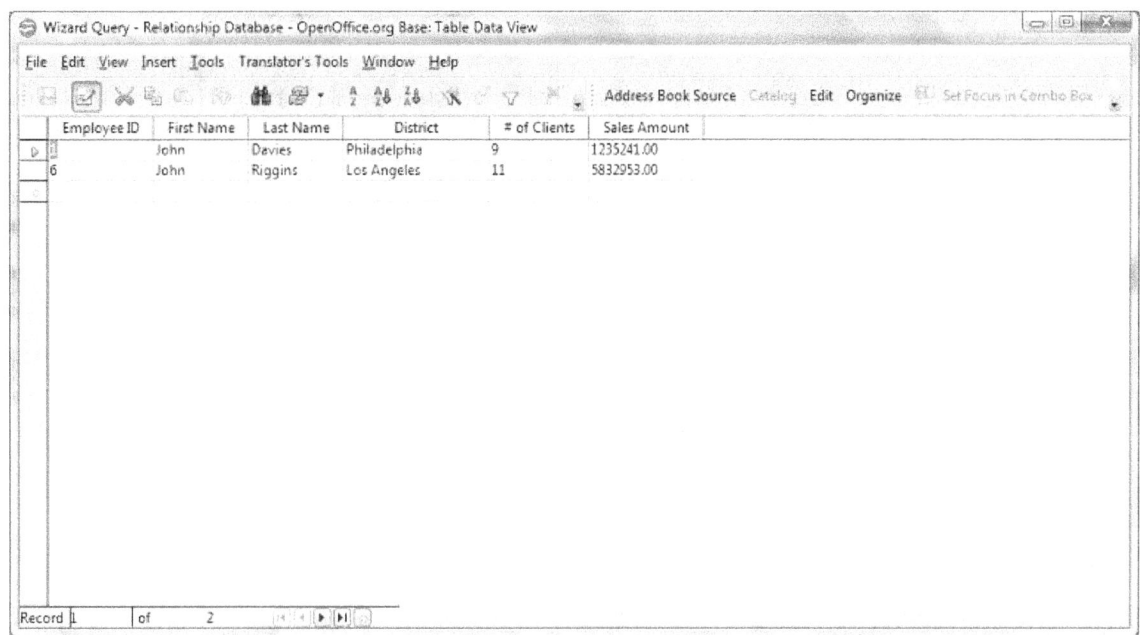

Figure 9

Note – Double-click the query in the **Queries** pane to run the query again at any time.

Figure 10

Growth & Assessment

1. How does the Wizard Query work?

2. In what screen do users have the ability to select the table that the fields will be pulled from and to then move those fields to be included in the query?

3. What occurs in the Sorting Order screen?

Section 3.7 – Using the Function Field

Section Objective:

- The Learn how to use the Function field when designing a Query.

Using the Function Field

OpenOffice Base has a feature referred to as the **Function field** which can perform a variety of mathematical functions. Mathematical functions, such as sum, count and average can be used in many situations and allow the user to do many things, such as test hypotheses, perform further analysis, or draw conclusions from a specific group of data. This section explains how a user can access this feature and perform some basic mathematical functions in OpenOffice Base.

Note – The steps below follow a specific example used to better instruct the user when working with this feature. Create a table in Base that contains the data shown in the figure below, and then perform Step 1.

Employee ID	First Name	Last Name	District	# of Clients	Sales Amount
1	John	Davies	Philadelphia	9	1235241.00
2	Ken	Paul	Philadelphia	7	1234234.00
3	Amy	Hoch	Pittsburgh	16	8342412.00
4	Chris	Mitchell	Pittsburgh	12	12312312.00
5	Josh	Flaim	Pittsburgh	14	7463134.00
6	John	Riggins	Los Angeles	11	5832953.00
7	Amy	Krallinger	Los Angeles	6	981573.00

Figure 1

Step 1: Click on the **Query** icon on the **Database** pane.

Figure 2

Step 2: Click the **Create Query in Design View…** on the **Tasks** pane. The Query window will open with the **Add Query or Table** dialog box displayed.

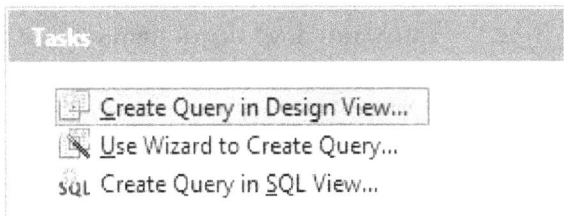

Figure 3

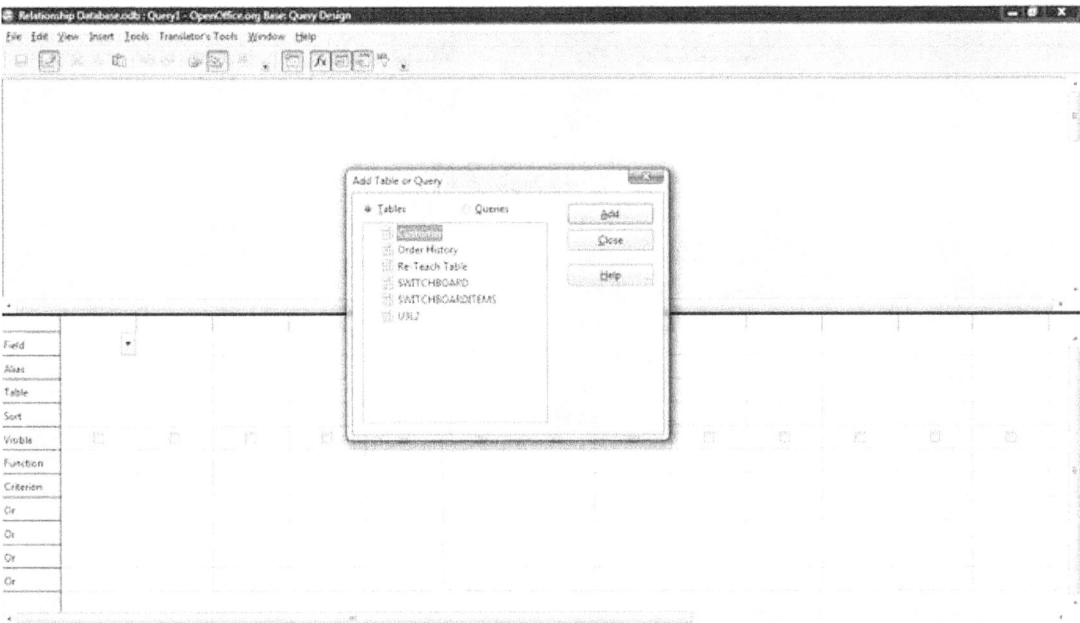

Figure 4

Step 3: Select the table that was created at the beginning of this section and then click **Add**. The table will be added to the Query.

Step 4: Click **Close** to exit the dialog box.

Step 5: Select **District** in the **Fields** drop-down menu, located in the first Query Designer column.

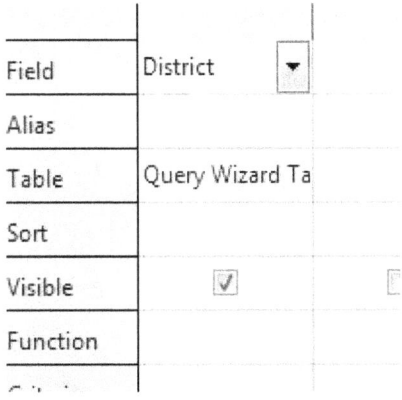

Figure 5

137

Step 6: Here, the user will work with the **Function field**. When functions are created with queries, the user must first select a field to group by. Since the user is finding the total sales for each district, the user must group together all occurrences of each district. This is done by selecting **Group by** from the **Function** drop-down menu in the **District** column.

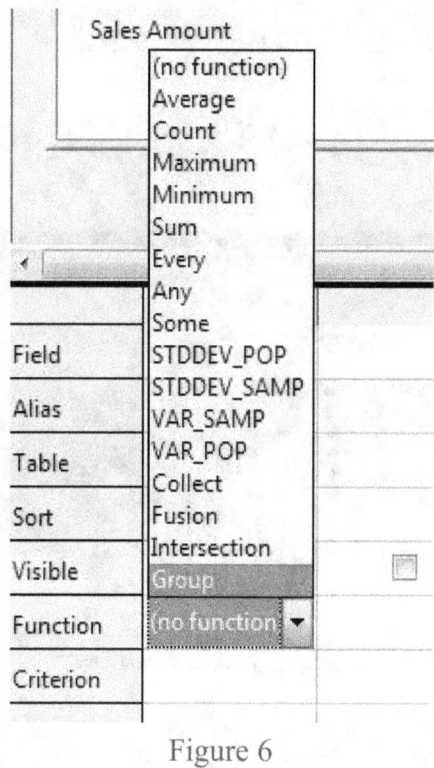

Figure 6

Step 7: In the second column, select **Sales Amount** from the **Field** drop-down menu.

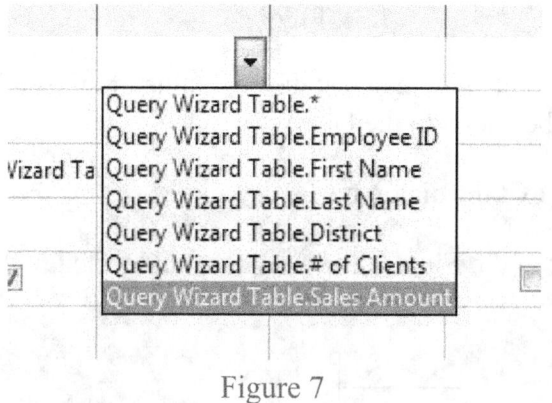

Figure 7

Step 8: Since the data is grouped by the District column, the user is able to perform a mathematical function in the **Sales Amount** field. From the **Function** drop-down menu, select **Sum**.

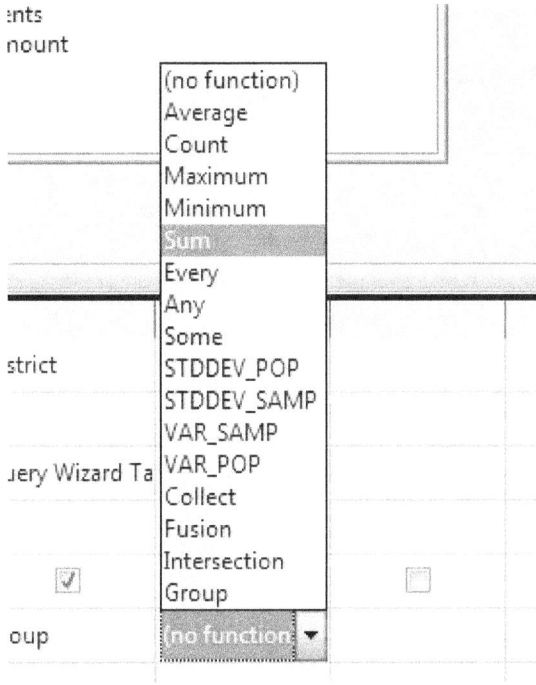

Figure 8

Step 9: Click the **Run Query** button to run the query. The results will be displayed.

Note – The keyboard shortcut **F5** will also run the query.

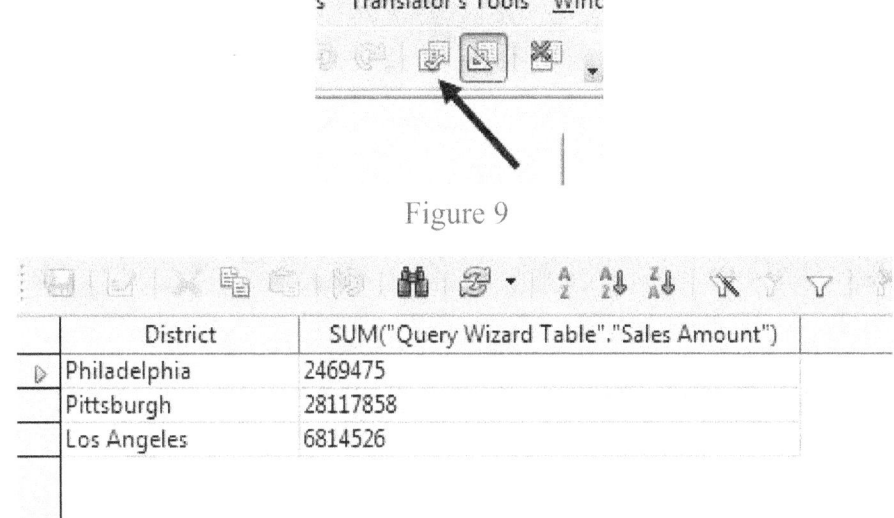

Figure 9

District	SUM("Query Wizard Table"."Sales Amount")
Philadelphia	2469475
Pittsburgh	28117858
Los Angeles	6814526

Figure 10

Take some time to create additional Queries using the sample table from this section to see the different mathematical functions available.

Growth & Assessment

1. What keyboard shortcut will also run the query?

2. What is the Function field used for?

3. One of the functions Function field can perform is "average."

Section 3.8 – Restricting Data Using Field Type Settings

Section Objective:

- Learn how to use Field Type settings to restrict data.

Restricting Data: Field Type

In OpenOffice Base, setting the field type will allow users to restrict the type of data that can be entered into a particular field. For example, fields with a data type that is set to **number** will only allow numerical values to be entered into the fields. The following steps outline how a user can set up field types to restrict unwanted data.

Step 1: Open a table in Design view.

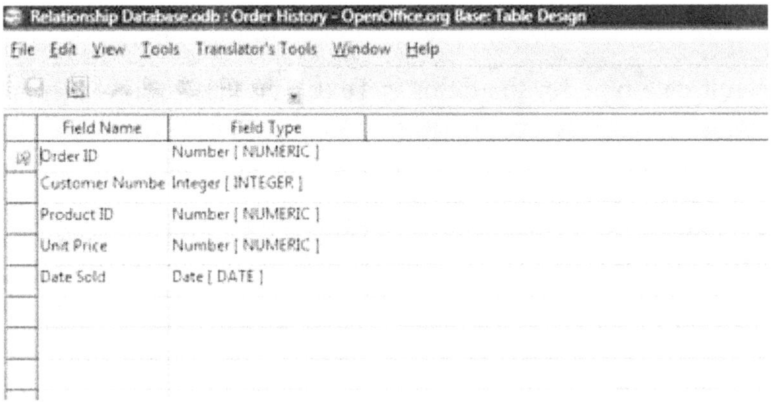

Figure 1

Step 2: Click in a particular field to modify its field type.

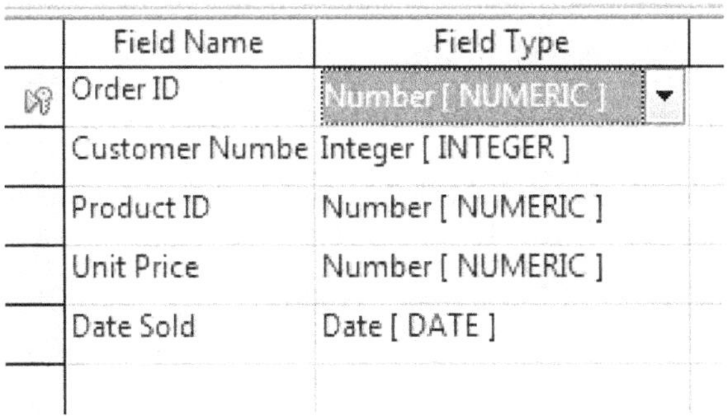

Figure 2

Step 3: Use the pull-down list to choose the preferred field type for the selected field.

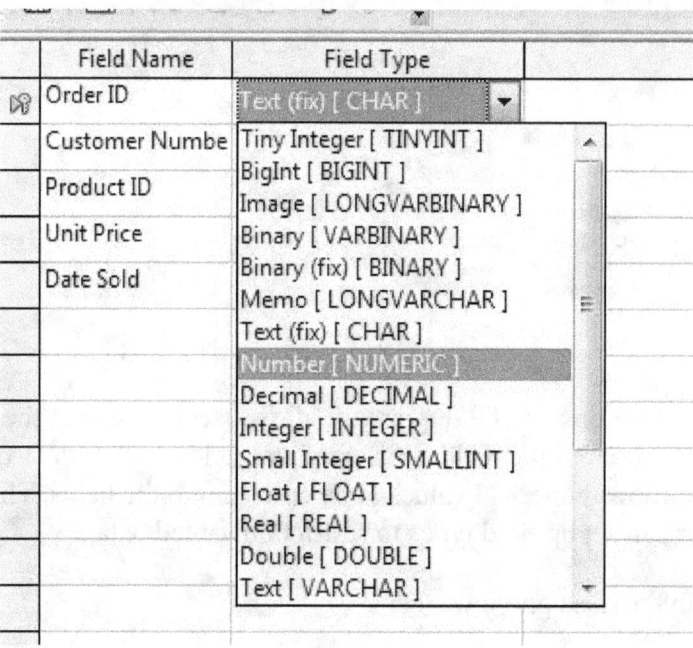

Figure 3

In Base, the default data type for the fields is **Text**. The table below displays some of the different field types that can be applied to the selected field. Once any of the field types have been chosen, only that specified field type will be accepted in the selected field.

Data Type	Description
Tiny Integer	A Tiny Integer is an integer that is 3 or less characters long.
BigInt	A Big Integer is an integer that is 19 or less characters long.
Text	A Text field can contain values that are text, numeric, or a combination of both. A text field can contain a maximum length of 255 characters.
Memo	A much larger version of the text field, allowing storage of up to 2 GB of data. A new feature of the OpenOffice Base Memo field is that it now supports rich text formatting.
Number	The Number field can store numeric values up to 16 bytes of data.
Date	The Date field allows storage of date information.
Time	The Time field allows for storage of time information
Currency	The Currency data type stores values in a monetary format. This can be used with financial data as 8-byte numbers with precision to four decimal places.
Yes/No	Boolean data storage of true/false values.
Date/Time	The Date/Time field is a timestamp field that will insert the current date and time when used

Growth & Assessment

1. What is a Tiny Integer?

2. A field with a data type that is set to number will only allow numerical values to be entered into the fields.

    a. TRUE

    b. FALSE

3. What is a BigInt?

4. What is the Yes/No data type also known as?

Section 3.9 – Restricting Data Using Field Length Settings

Section Objective:

- Learn how to use Field Length settings to restrict data.

Restricting Data: Field Length

In OpenOffice Base, when working with Text and Numerical Data Types, users are allowed to restrict the size of the data that can be entered into a particular field. This is useful if numerical values are being entered into the table and a single number cannot exceed a certain amount. The following steps outline how a user can set up these types of restrictions.

Step 1: Open a table in **Design** view.

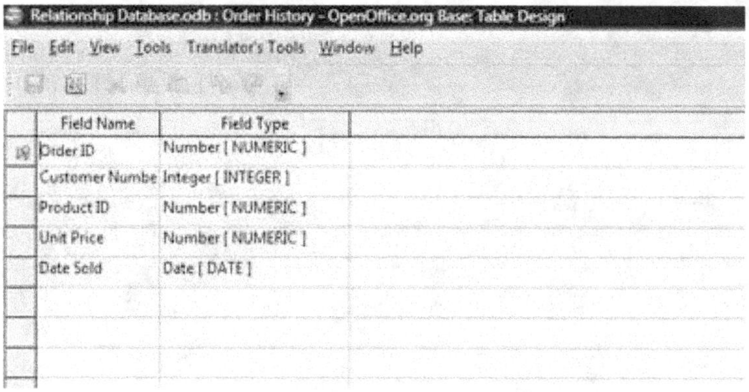

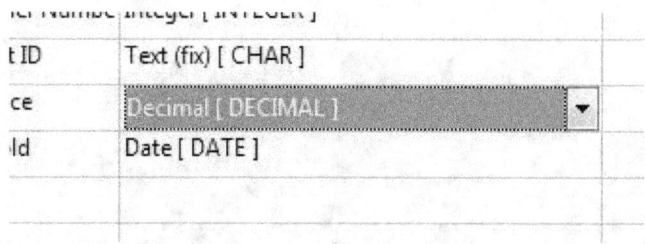

Figure 1

Step 2: Click in a particular field to modify its Field Size.

Figure 2

Step 3: In the **Field Properties** window, located at the bottom of the screen, click the **Length** box.

Figure 3

Step 4: There will be a default value of **255** Characters for text, and **10** Integers for numbers. Change the default by doing the following:

- **For Text** – Type a value from 1-255 in the **Length** box. The number entered will be the maximum number of characters that will be permitted.

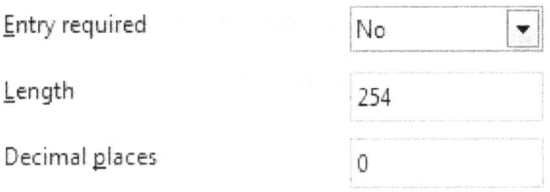

Figure 4

- **For Numbers** – Change the value in the textbox from 10 to any number greater than 1, or choose a different type of Numerical value which will have its own default value.

Once the Field Size has been specified, no data that exceeds that size will be allowed in the selected field.

Growth & Assessment

1. What is the default value for Length of text?

2. Users are able to restrict the size of the data that can be entered into a specific field.

    a. TRUE

    b. FALSE

3. Why is it useful to be able to restrict the size of data?

Section 3.10 – Creating a Report

Section Objective:

- Learn about the three basic sections of every Report: Report Header, Detail, and Report Footer.
- Learn how to create a Report.

Creating a Report

In OpenOffice Base, an important part of becoming comfortable with the application is learning how to create Reports using the data found within the tables. A Report is a specialized database that contains objects that make it easier to review and edit. There are three basic sections found within every Report: the **Report Header**, the **Report Detail**, and the **Report Footer**. This section will describe these three aspects of the Report.

The Report Header

The **Report Header** acts like the header for any other item that may be created in the OpenOffice Suite. It is located at the top of each record within a Report. The Header can be accessed through the **Header** grouping located in the **Insert** drop-down menu. Some common items that can be added to a Report Header are the title of the Report or database, the date, and a company or school logo.

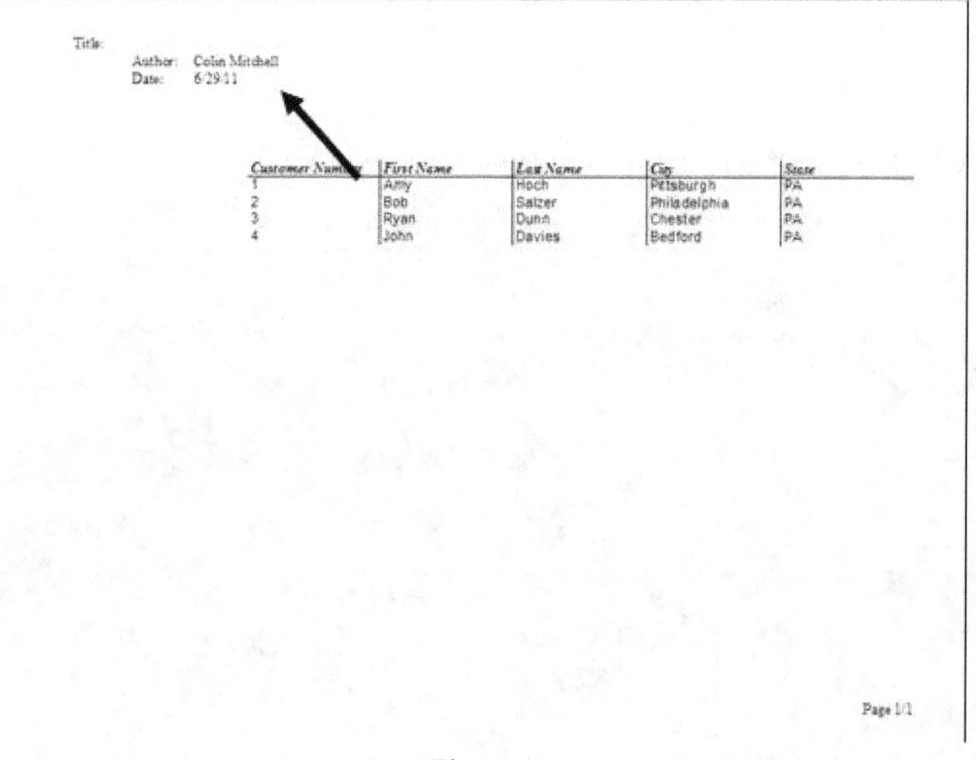

Figure 1

Report Detail

Every Report will contain a **Report Detail** section. The Report Detail section is accessed when a user creates a Report in Design view. The Detail section allows the user to choose which fields will be used as part of the Report by selecting the desired fields from the **Field List**.

The Detail section will have a grid where the user has the ability to place additional controls to enhance the Report. The grid can be deleted by clicking the **Show Grid** command in the **Report Design** toolbar at the bottom of the screen.

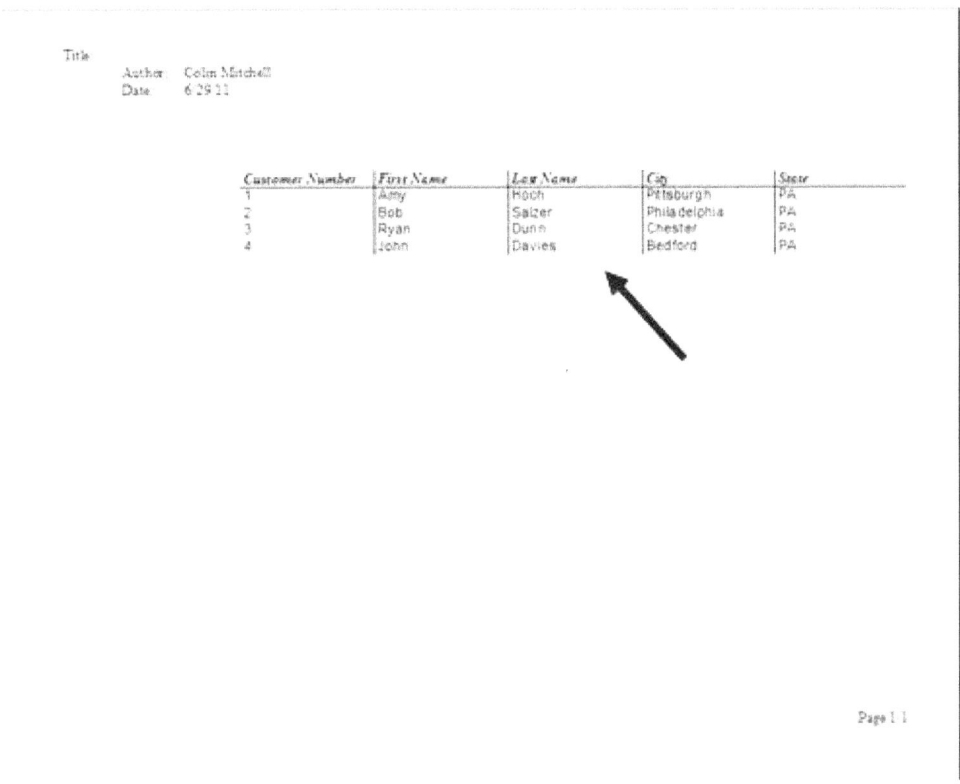

Figure 2

Report Footer

The **Report Footer** is very similar to the Report Header except it is at the bottom of the screen instead of the top. The Footer can be accessed through the **Footer** grouping located in the **Insert** drop-down menu. The user is able to add the same information in the Footer as they are able to add in the Header; by default however, Base will add the **Page Number** as a right aligned data item in the Footer.

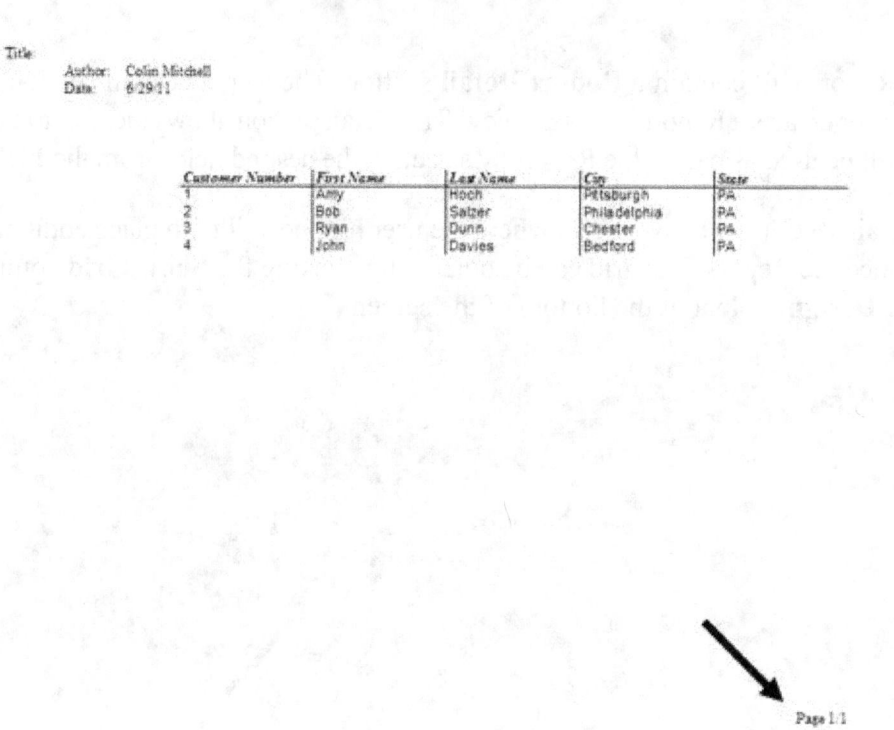

Figure 3

Growth & Assessment

1. What is the Report Footer?

2. How is the Footer accessed?

3. What does the Report Detail section allow users to do?

4. The Report Header acts like the header for any other item that may be created in the OpenOffice Suite.

   a. TRUE

   b. FALSE

Section 3.11 – Creating a Report Using the Report Wizard

Section Objective:

- Learn to create a Report using the Report Wizard.

Report Wizard

When working in OpenOffice Base, it is convenient to have a database contain all of the data needed because it is all in one place for when a user needs to reference the collected data or generated figures; however, having all of the collected data isn't the most convenient when presenting the data to others. The solution to this problem is to create a Base Report which allows the user to design a ready-to-print document containing the desired database information. The Report Wizard, like other application wizards, provides descriptive and informative steps that guide the user through the process of adding fields and a design to a Report.

Before following the steps below, create a new database table containing the information presented in the figure below.

Employee ID	First Name	Last Name	District	# of Clients	Sales Amount
1	John	Davies	Philadelphia	9	1235241.00
2	Ken	Paul	Philadelphia	7	1234234.00
3	Amy	Hoch	Pittsburgh	16	8342412.00
4	Chris	Mitchell	Pittsburgh	12	12312312.00
5	Josh	Flaim	Pittsburgh	14	7463134.00
6	John	Riggins	Los Angeles	11	5832953.00
7	Amy	Krallinger	Los Angeles	6	981573.00

Figure 1

Step 1: Click on the **Reports** icon found on the **Database** pane, which is located along the left side of the application window.

Figure 2

Step 2: Double-click on **Use Wizard to Create Report…** found in the **Tasks** pane at the top of the application window. The **Report Wizard** dialog box will appear.

Figure 3

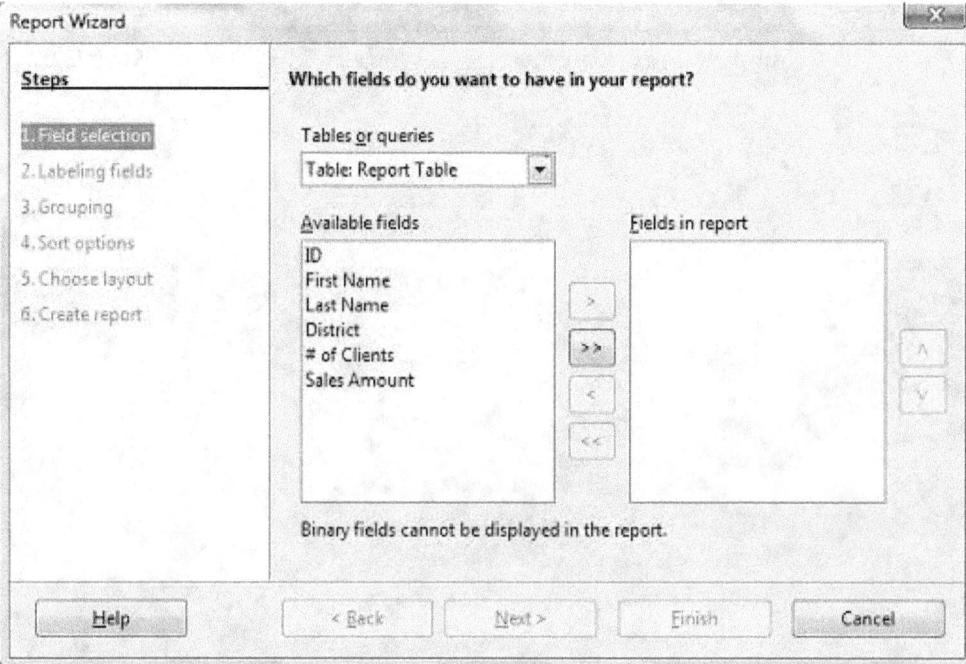

Figure 4

Step 3: The first page of the wizard is where the user has the ability to choose the fields that will be displayed in the report. First, select a table to reference from the drop-down menu. Once a table has been selected, choose which fields from that table will be included. For this example, select the table previously created and click the **>>** button to move all of the fields into the **Fields in Report** window. Once the required fields have been added, click the **Next** button to move to the next page of the wizard.

Figure 5

Note – Base allows users to use multiple tables when creating a report.

Step 4: The next page of the wizard is where the user can modify the labels that will be displayed for each of the fields added to the report. For this example, add spaces between AccountID, FirstName, etc. Once these changes have been made to the labels, click **Next** to move to the next page of the wizard.

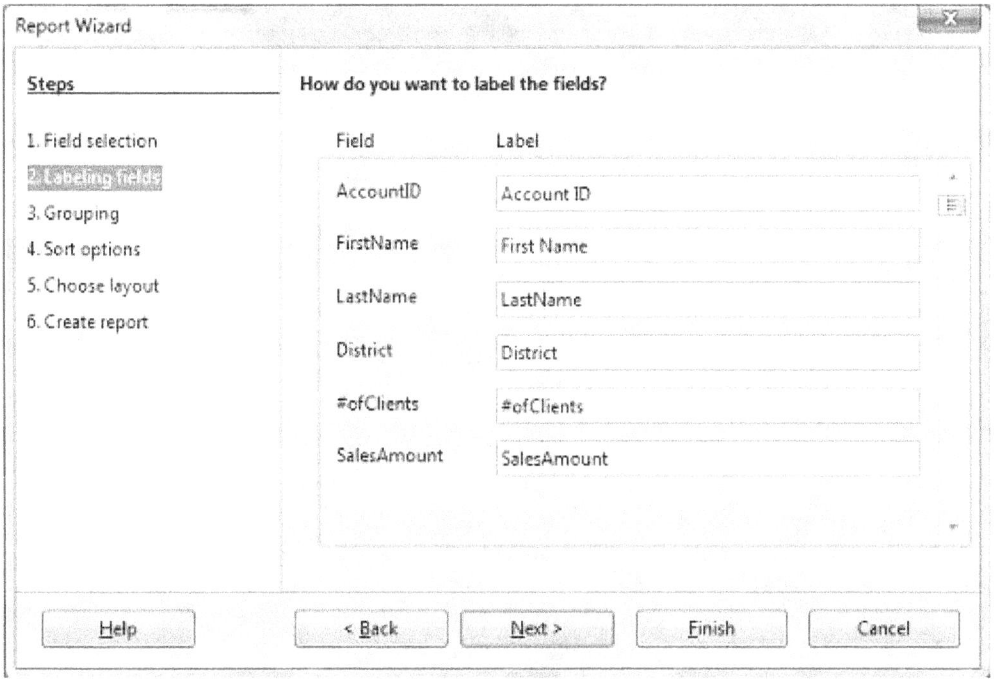

Figure 6

Step 5: The third page of the wizard allows the user to add **grouping levels** to the report. An example of a grouping level would be if a user decided to group by region. If a user grouped by region then all of the records would be placed under their particular region name. An example of a grouped report is displayed below.

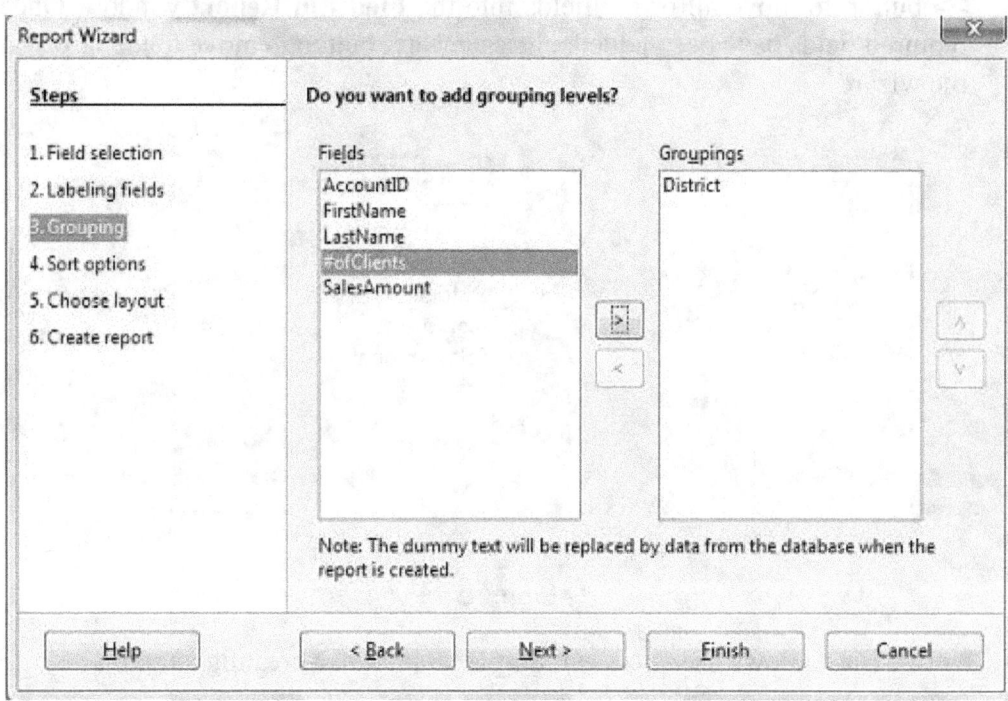

Figure 7

For this particular example, move **Region** over to the **Groupings** window using the > button. When the changes have been made, click **Next** to move to the next page of the wizard.

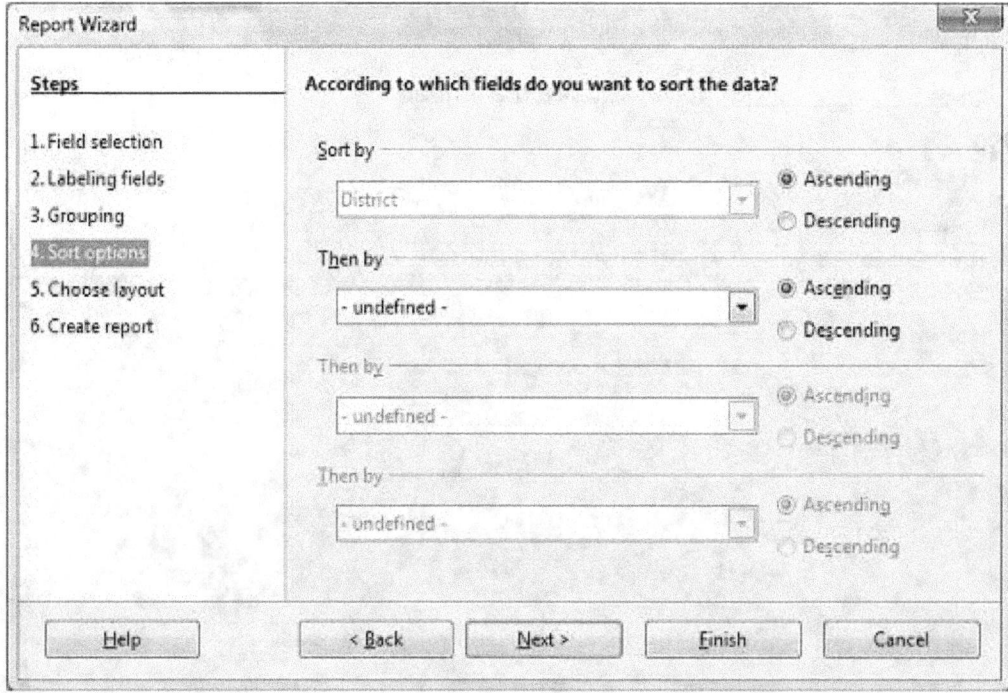

Figure 8

152

Step 6: The next page of the wizard allows the user to apply additional sorting to the records displayed in the Report. If groupings have been made on the previous screen, the field that was used for grouping will automatically have a **Sort field** set up for it. To add additional sorting, select the desired field to sort in the drop-down menu, and click the radio button next to either **Ascending** or **Descending**. Once the desired fields have had an additional sort applied to them, click **Next** to move onto the next page of the wizard.

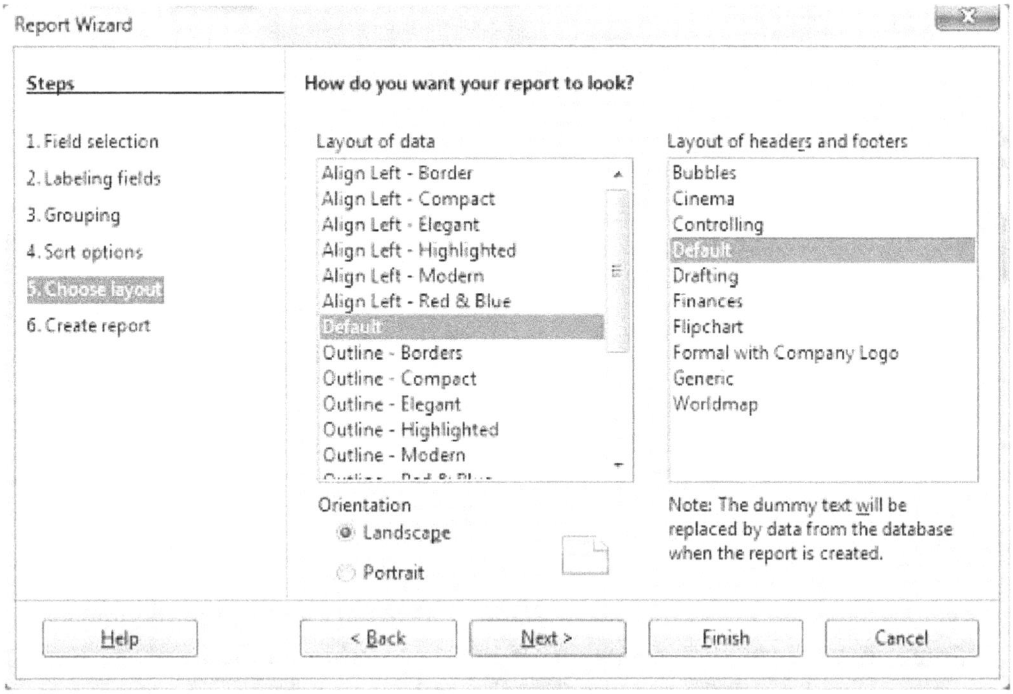

Figure 9

Step 7: The **Choose Layout** page of the wizard is separated into three parts, which are explained below:

- **Layout of data** – This section determines how the Detail portion of the Report is laid out on the screen. The user is able to click through different options and automatically see a preview of the Report page. For this example, select **Outline–Borders**.

- **Layouts of headers and footers** – This section will determine the design of the **Report Header** and **Report Footer**. As with the data section, clicking on one of these options will automatically cause a preview to appear in the Report window. For this example, select **Controlling**.

- **Orientation** – Click on either the **Landscape** or **Portrait** radio buttons to determine the direction in which the Report is displayed on the page. For this example, select **Landscape**.

Once all of the necessary selections have been made, click the **Next** button to go to the final page of the Report Wizard.

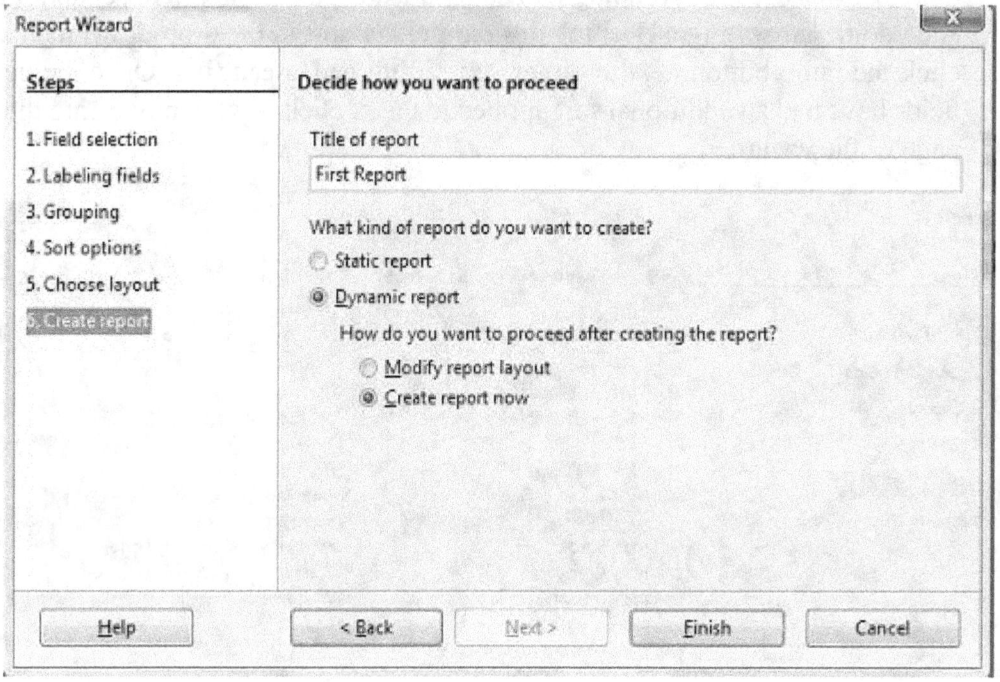

Figure 10

Step 8: The final page of the wizard is where the user names the report and determines whether it should be Dynamic or Static. A **Dynamic** report will be updated every time it is viewed. This means that if the data within the fields of the Report has been updated, the Report will reflect the updated data every time the Report is refreshed and viewed. If the report is **Static**, then it will never be updated and it will stay exactly as it is when run, regardless of any updates to the source data. For this example, name the Report "**First Report**" and leave the report style as **Dynamic**, which is the default.

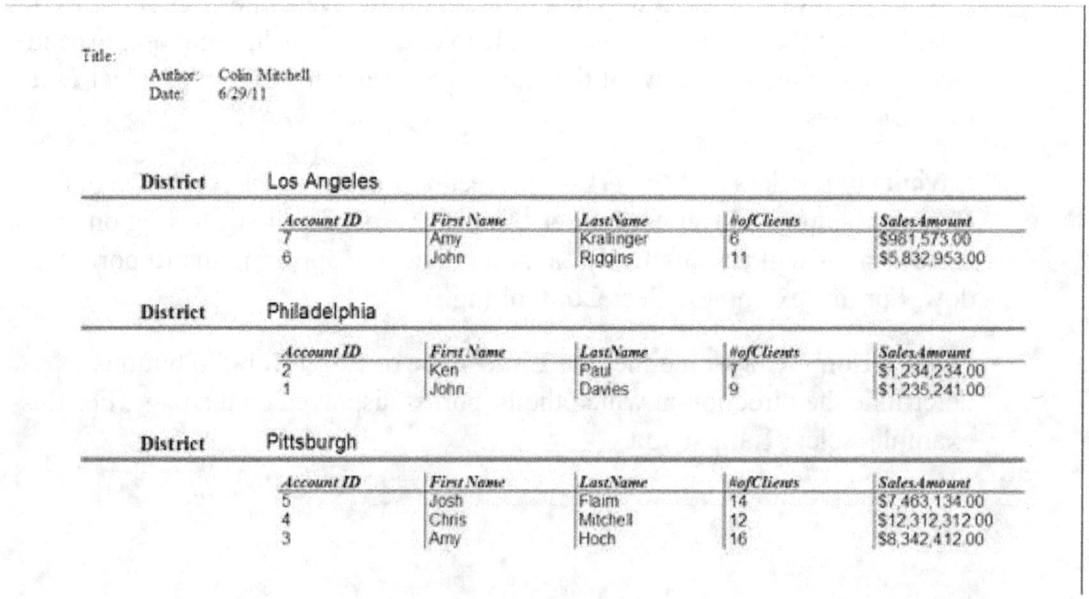

Title:

Author: Colin Mitchell
Date: 6/29/11

District Los Angeles

Account ID	First Name	LastName	#ofClients	SalesAmount
7	Amy	Kralinger	6	$981,573.00
6	John	Riggins	11	$5,832,953.00

District Philadelphia

Account ID	First Name	LastName	#ofClients	SalesAmount
2	Ken	Paul	7	$1,234,234.00
1	John	Davies	9	$1,235,241.00

District Pittsburgh

Account ID	First Name	LastName	#ofClients	SalesAmount
5	Josh	Flaim	14	$7,463,134.00
4	Chris	Mitchell	12	$12,312,312.00
3	Amy	Hoch	16	$8,342,412.00

Figure 11

Step 9: Click the **Finish** button. The created Report will be displayed on the screen.

Growth & Assessment

1. How many parts is the Choose Layout section of the wizard separated into?

2. What are the parts of the Choose Layout section of the wizard?

3. A Dynamic report will be updated every other time it is viewed.

    a. TRUE

    b. FALSE

4. What is the Orientation option within the wizard used for?

Section 3.12 – Changing the Font, Size, and Color of the Text

Section Objective:

- Learn how to change the look of text.

Changing the Text

OpenOffice Base allows users to change the **Font**, **Size**, and **Color** of the text in a Form from the **Toolbar**, or from the **Character** dialog box. Accessing these tools from the Toolbar allows the user to make modifications to the text quickly while working in the application. The Character dialog box is helpful when formatting a large amount of text. The following steps outline how both of these are done.

Formatting Text through the Toolbar

Step 1: Select the desired field to be formatted.

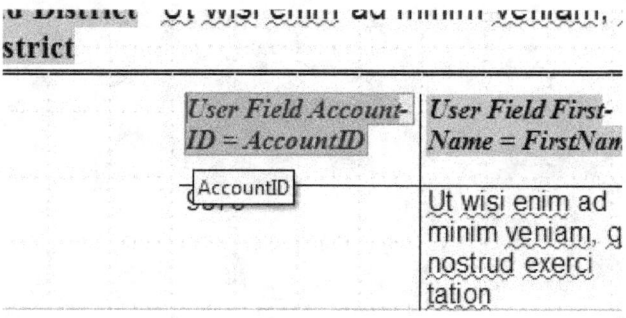

Figure 1

Step 2: From the **Formatting Toolbar**, click the arrow next to the **Font** textbox. A drop-down menu with the **Font options** will appear.

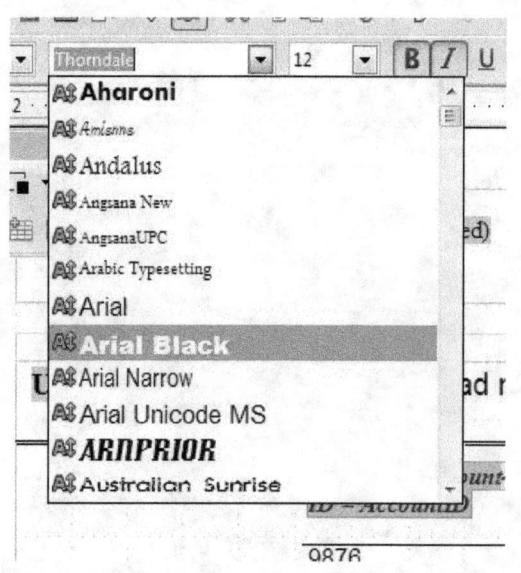

Figure 2

Step 3: From the **Font** drop-down menu, select the preferred font. The font will automatically be applied to the text within the selected field.

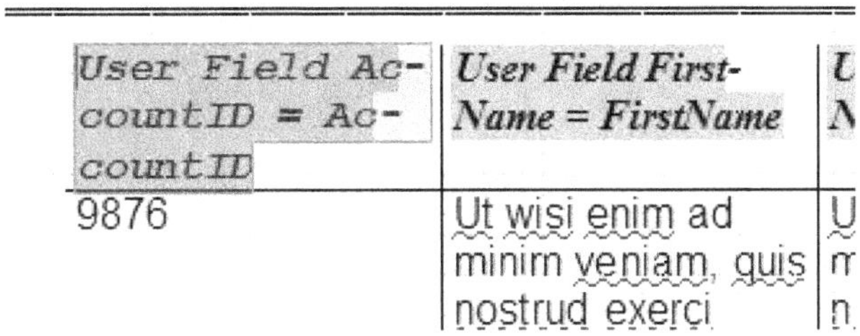

Figure 3

Step 4: To select a different size, access the **Font Size** pull-down list and select the preferred size.

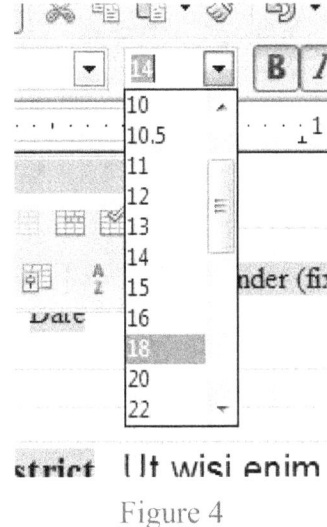

Figure 4

Step 5: To select a different color, click the arrow next to **Font Color** and select the preferred color.

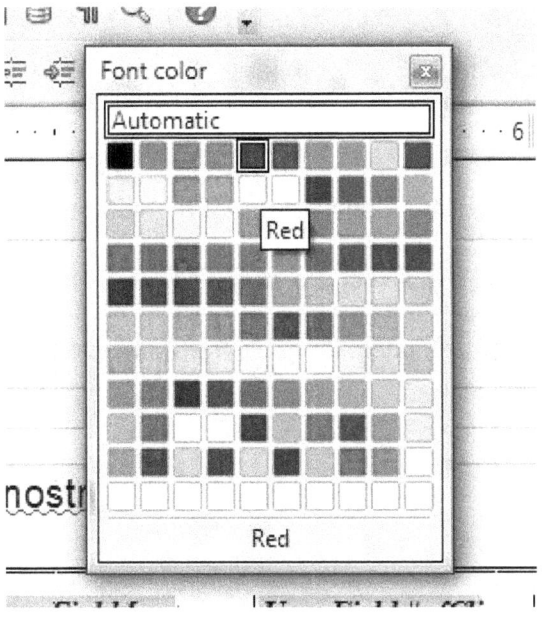

Figure 5

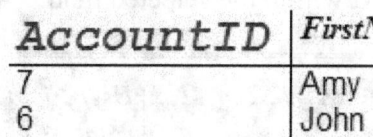

Figure 6

Formatting Text through the Character Dialog Box

Step 1: Highlight the desired text.

Step 2: Select **Format**, located on the Menu Bar.

Step 3: From the Format drop-down menu, click **Character…**. The **Character** dialog box will appear.

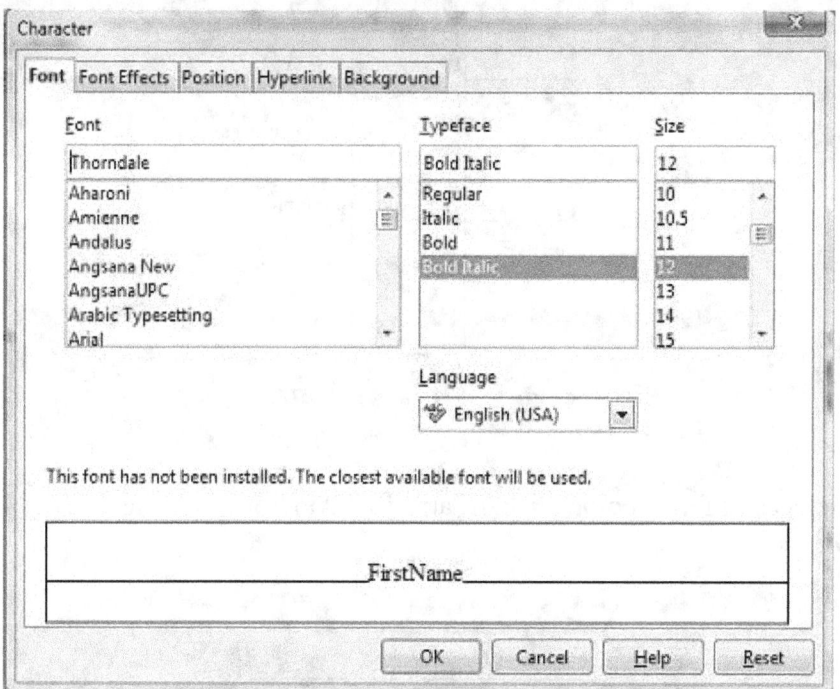

Figure 7

Step 4: Click the **Font** tab located along the top of the window.

Step 5: From the **Font** scroll list, select the preferred font.

Step 6: From the **Size** scroll list, select the preferred font size.

Step 7: Click on the **Font Effects** tab.

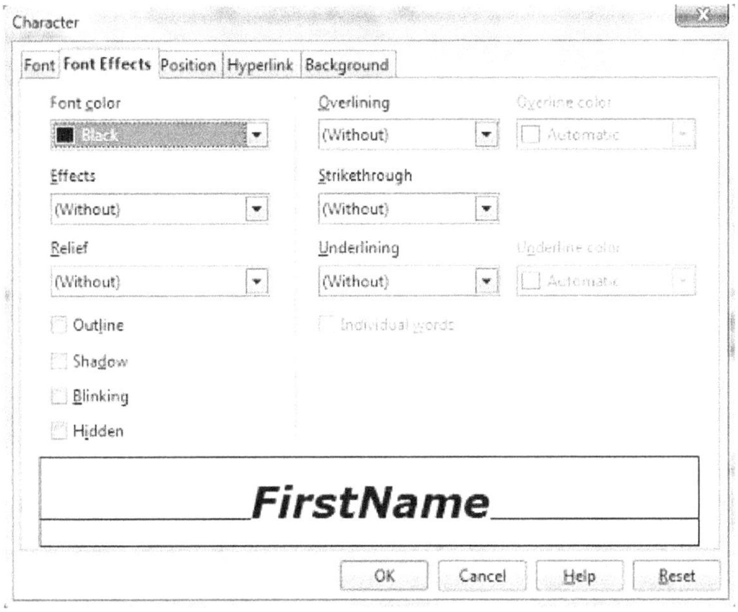

Figure 8

Step 8: In the **Font Color** drop-down menu, select the preferred font color.

Step 9: Click **OK**. The changes will be applied to the selected text.

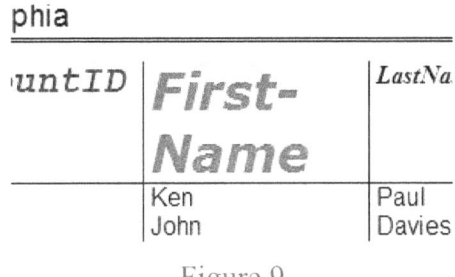

Figure 9

Growth & Assessment

1. OpenOffice Base allows the user to change the Font, Size, and Color of the text in a Form from the Toolbar.

    a. TRUE

    b. FALSE

2. What is the other option to choose from when changing Font, Size, and Color?

3. The Character dialog box is helpful when formatting a large amount of text.

    a. TRUE

    b. FALSE

Section 3.13 – Restricting Data Using the Combo Box

Section Objective:

- Learn to add a Combo Box to a Form to restrict data.

Restricting Data: Combo Box

In OpenOffice Base, the **Combo Box** combines the features of a textbox and a list box. It does this by allowing users to select an item either by typing text into the Combo Box, or by selecting it from a list using values that have been previously set up. If the number of items exceeds what can be displayed in the Combo Box, scroll bars will automatically appear on the feature. The user is able to scroll up and down, or left to right through the list. The following steps outline how to access and use the Combo Box to restrict unwanted data.

Step 1: Open a form in **Design** view.

Step 2: Click **View**, located on the Menu Bar.

Step 3: From the View drop-down menu, scroll over **Toolbars** and select **Form Controls**. The **Form Controls** toolbar will appear vertically on the left side of the screen.

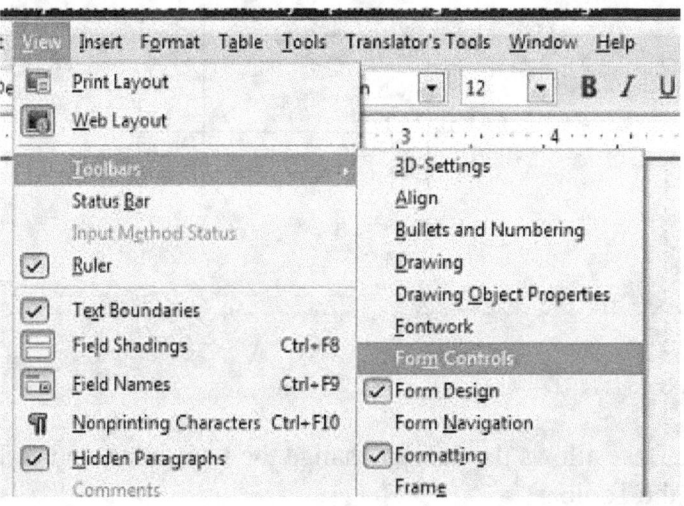

Figure 1

Figure 2

Step 4: Click the icon for the **Combo Box** control.

Figure 3

Step 5: In the Form design grid, position the top left-hand corner of the Combo Box in the desired position and hold down the left mouse button. While holding down the left mouse button, drag the cursor to where the other edge of the control field is needed and then release the left mouse button. The Combo Box will be inserted into the Form and the **Combo Box Wizard** will open.

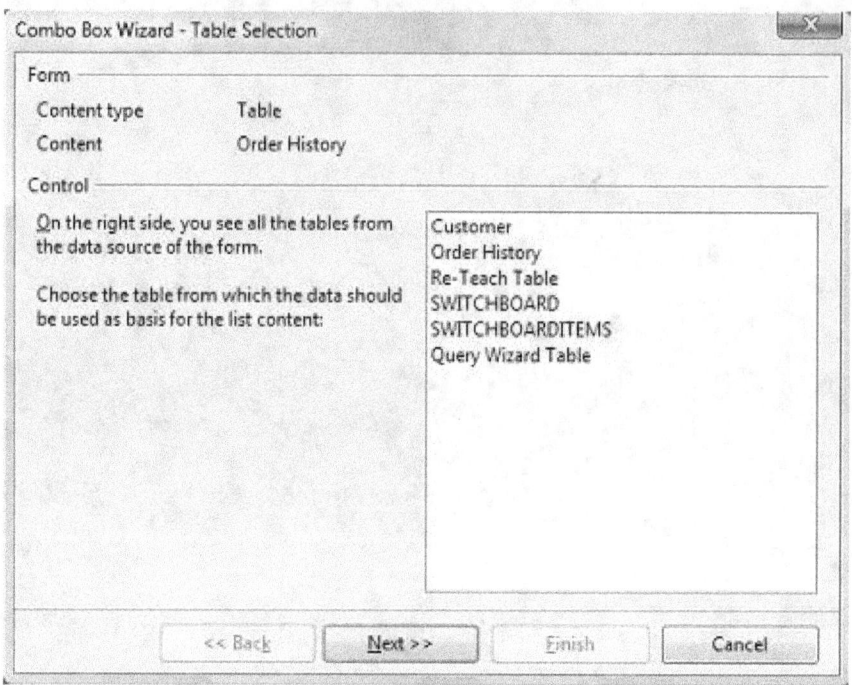

Figure 4

Step 6: The first page of the wizard is where the user selects the table that will be used to base the Combo Box off of. Any of the tables that have been previously created in the database will be available. Choose the preferred table and then click the **Next** button.

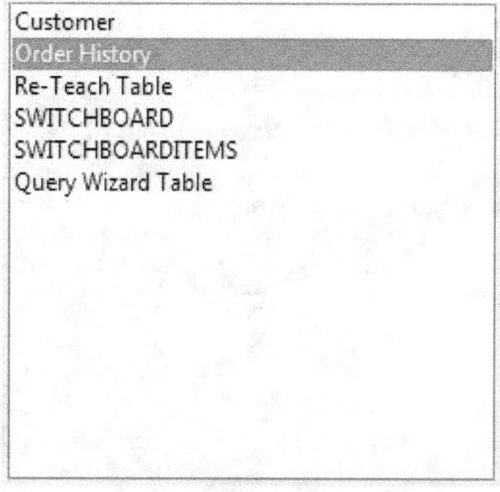

Figure 5

Step 7: The next page of the wizard is where the field, with the preferred contents, is selected to be shown in the Combo Box list. After selecting the preferred field, click the **Next** button.

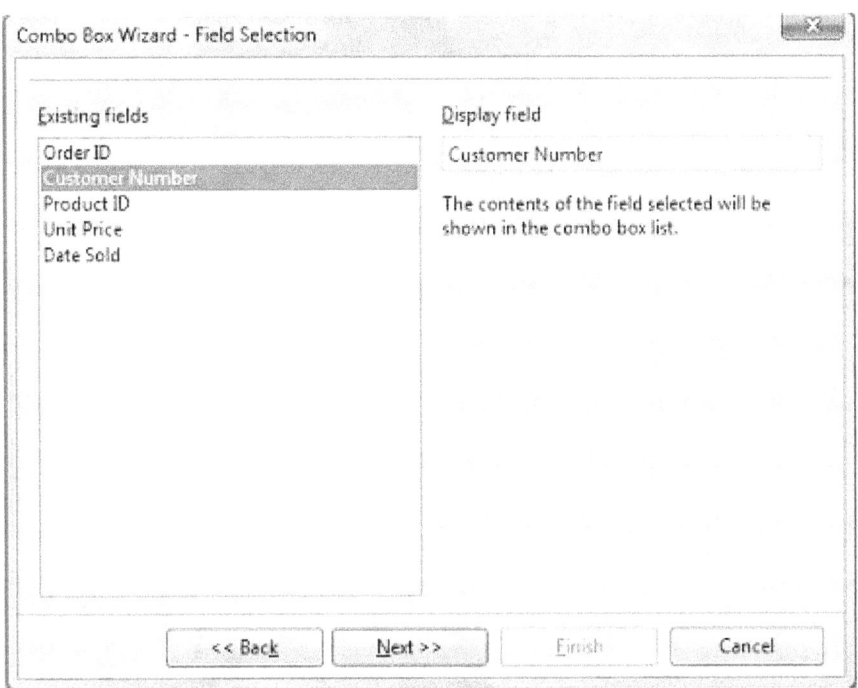

Figure 6

Step 8: The third page of the wizard is where the user decides if they want the Combo Box value saved into the table (the table in which the Combo Box is created from), or if they would like the Combo Box value only saved in the Form. In most instances, the user will not want to have the selections added to the table, so select the radio button to only save the selection in the Form.

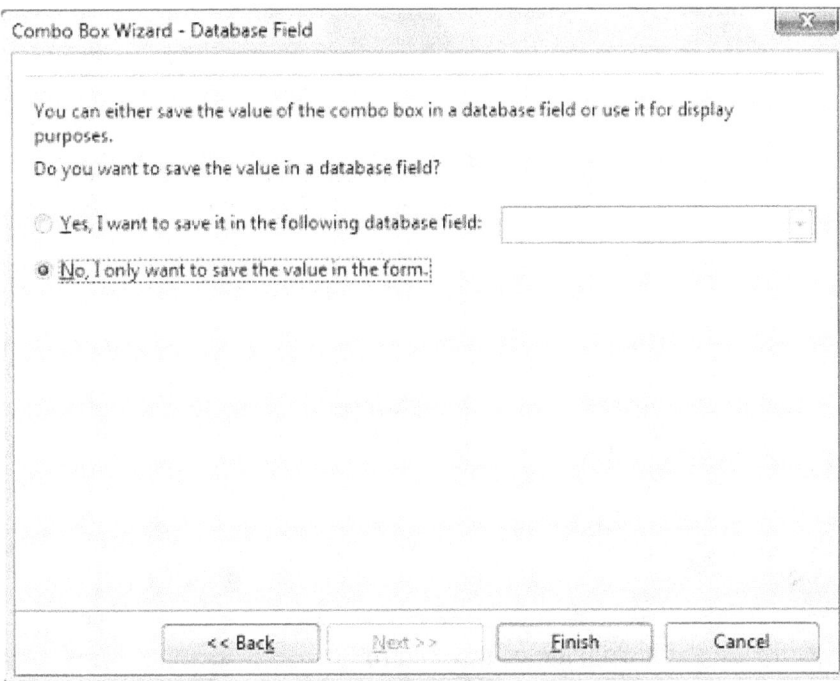

Figure 7

Step 9: Click the **Finish** button to exit the wizard. The Combo Box will be inserted into the Form.

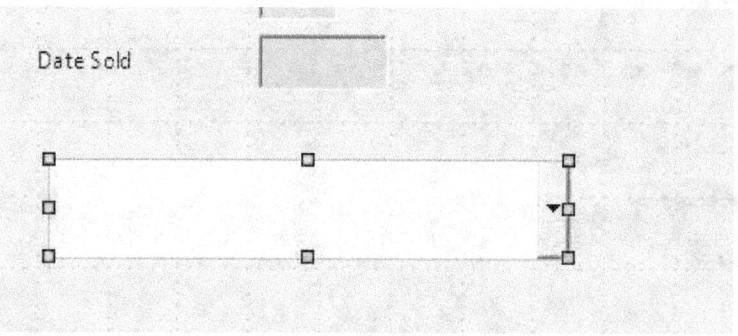

Figure 8

Step 10: Click on the arrow found on the Combo Box to expand it and view the available options for selections.

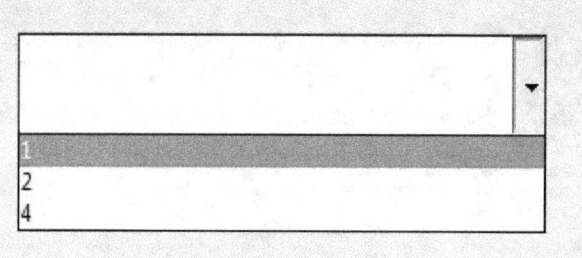

Figure 9

Note – If no available options are desired in the drop-down menu, the user has the option to manually type in the preferred value.

Figure 10

Growth & Assessment

1. If no available options are desired in the drop-down menu, the user has the option to manually type in the preferred value.

    a. TRUE

    b. FALSE

2. What occurs on the third page of the wizard?

3. What does the Combo Box combine?

Section 3.14 – Updating Information within a Table

Section Objective:

- Learn how to update information in a table.

Updating Information

When working in OpenOffice Base, there are times when certain information needs to be updated. Users can edit an existing record by opening a table and navigating to the desired record. Once there, they can make any necessary updates to the information. The steps below describe this process in greater detail.

Step 1: Open an existing Base table in Data View.

Customer Number	First Name	Last Name	City	State
1	Amy	Mitchell	Pittsburgh	PA
2	Bob	Salzer	Philadelphia	PA
3	Ryan	Dunn	Chester	PA
4	John	Davies	Bedford	PA

Figure 1

Note – Make sure the **Edit Data** button on the Toolbar is selected. If it is not, the table will be locked and the user will be unable to make any modifications.

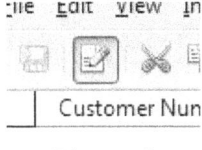

Figure 2

Step 2: Select the contents of the field that are to be replaced.

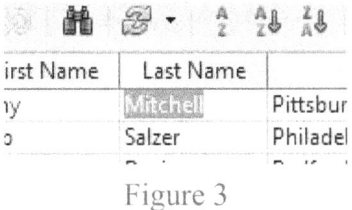

Figure 3

Step 3: Type or select the new value for the field.

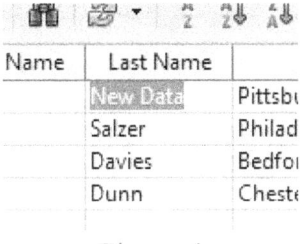

Figure 4

Growth & Assessment

1. Users are unable to edit an existing record in Base.

    a. TRUE

    b. FALSE

2. What button must be selected on the Toolbar to unlock the table?

3. Data can be easily and quickly edited within a table as long as the Edit Table button is selected.

    a. TRUE

    b. FALSE

Section 3.15 – Deleting Information within a Table

Section Objective:

- Learn how to delete information from a table.

Deleting Information

Base, like the rest of the OpenOffice.org Suite, allows users to delete data at any time. In this particular application, users have the ability to delete the data in individual fields when the tables open in Data view. The following steps outline how this is done.

Step 1: Open an existing Base table in Data View.

Customer Number	First Name	Last Name	City	State
1	Amy	Mitchell	Pittsburgh	PA
2	Bob	Salzer	Philadelphia	PA
3	Ryan	Dunn	Chester	PA
4	John	Davies	Bedford	PA

Figure 1

Note – Make sure the **Edit Data** button on the Toolbar is selected. If it is not, the table will be locked and the user will be unable to make any modifications.

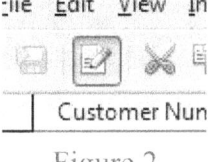

Figure 2

Step 2: Select the data that needs to be deleted.

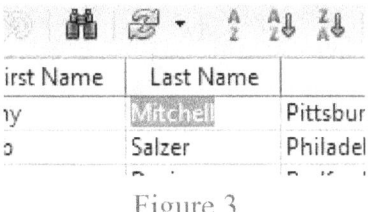

Figure 3

167

Step 4: Right-click anywhere within the highlighted cell. The **Quick Menu** will appear.

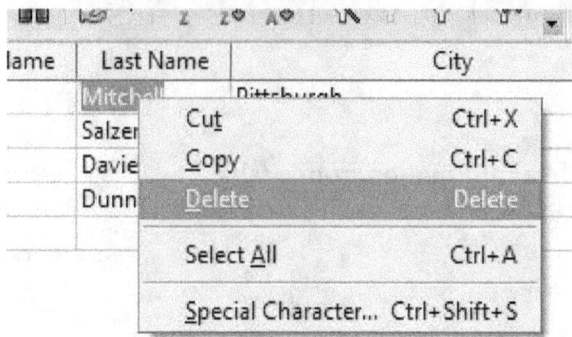

Figure 4

Step 5: Select **Delete** from the Quick Menu. The selected data will be removed from the highlighted cell.

Note – The **DELETE** or **BACKSPACE** keys also delete the contents of a cell.

Growth & Assessment

1. What two keys are used to delete the contents of a cell?

2. Users are unable to delete selected data within Base by using the DELETE or BACKSPACE keys.

    a. TRUE

    b. FALSE

3. What is the purpose of the Edit Data button?

Appendix

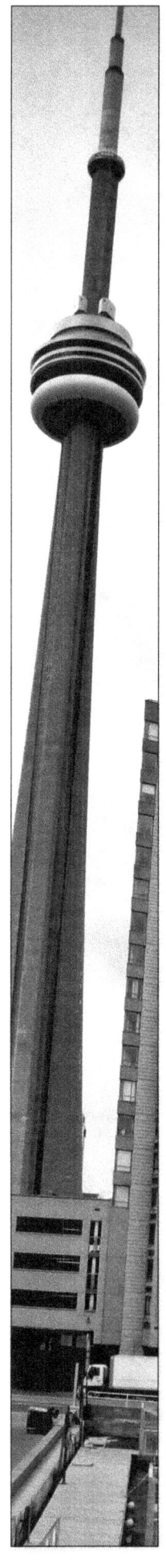

OpenOffice Volume III: Base Unit 1

Section 1.1

1. Six

2. a. TRUE

3. Modules are files that contain Visual Basic code.

4. Forms provide an easy way to view or change the information in a table

Section 1.2

1. a. TRUE

2. Data and Design

3. Design view allows the user to create or modify a table, form, or other database object, as well as configure the fields.

Section 1.3

1. a. TRUE

2. The Database Wizard dialog box.

3. Whether the new database should open for manual editing (default selection), or if the new database should open by creating tables using a wizard.

4. The Save As dialog box.

Section 1.4

1. Automatically Add a Primary Key, Use an Existing Field as a Primary Key, Define Primary Key as a Combination of Several Fields

2. A primary key is a field, or set of fields, with a unique value for each record stored in the table.

3. Selecting whether the table is for business or personal purposes.

Section 1.5

1. a. TRUE

2. To provide a description of what the user is working with within the database

3. Text[VARCHAR]

4. Three

Section 1.6

1. a. TRUE

2. Clicking the diskette icon in the upper left corner of the toolbar.

3. In the Database pane.

Section 1.7

1. Three

2. a. TRUE

3. Select Open to show the Open dialog box. Using the Open dialog box, browse for the OpenOffice Base database file.

Section 1.8

1. a. TRUE

2. CTRL + S

3. a. TRUE

4. Selecting Save All

Section 1.9

1. Primary keys are important because they prevent the user from having duplicate records within the table.

2. a. TRUE

3. b. FALSE

4. Design and Data

Section 1.10

1. When a user clicks somewhere else.

2. a. TRUE

3. To show extended tips about the buttons available on the application's different toolbars

Section 1.11

1. a. TRUE

2. Move the mouse to the right edge of the column to be modified. Drag left to shrink the column, or drag right to make the column wider.

3. Right-click heading of the column to be modified and select Column Width. Enter the column width that is needed and click **OK**.

Section 1.12

1. a. TRUE

2. The user will not be able to supply a value for the specific field.

3. Right-click any column header and choose **Show Columns.**

4. b. FALSE

Section 1.13

1. a. TRUE

2. The column cell will automatically format itself to the width of the widest entry.

3. b. FALSE

Section 1.14

1. a. TRUE

2. Create button

3. It's helpful when a user has created a mass amount of data in an OpenOffice Calc spreadsheet and wishes to analyze the data further using the tools and features in Base.

Section 1.15

1. b. FALSE

2. All fields will move to the right side of the window

3. The **Insert Database Columns** window

OpenOffice Volume III: Base Unit 2

Section 2.1

1. A Database Application is a collection of records or data.

2. Controls are buttons, links, lists, and other pieces of user interface that you can be added to forms.

3. a. TRUE

4. Command buttons provide a way of performing actions by clicking them.

Section 2.2

1. The Open Database Object button on the Toolbar

2. a. TRUE

3. A confirmation pop-up will open.

4. a. TRUE

Section 2.3

1. The Arrange controls step is where the user has the ability to choose how the form controls will be displayed on the screen. Database Application is a collection of records or data.

2. a. TRUE

3. b. FALSE

4. Borders and background color are chosen for the form

175

Section 2.4

1. A form
2. It allows the user to navigate through, or perform tasks within, the application
3. Any of the following: opening other forms, running queries, printing reports

Section 2.5

1. a. TRUE
2. The property sheet
3. a. TRUE
4. The Properties dialog box

Section 2.6

1. CTRL + A
2. To reduce user error
3. …
4. b. FALSE

Section 2.7

1. a. TRUE
2. One box shows the old color and one shows the new color.
3. It adds visual appeal.
4. a. TRUE

Section 2.8

1. Close the dialog box
2. b. FALSE
3. The Form Design toolbar

Section 2.9

1. Provides the user with two views of the database at the same time
2. Table in Data view and an original Form
3. a. TRUE
4. b. FALSE

Section 2.10

1. Textbox
2. Form Design grid
3. a. TRUE

Section 2.11

1. a. TRUE
2. Displays a list of items the user can from
3. b. FALSE

Section 2.12

1. Three
2. a. TRUE
3. The field is permanently removed from the form.
4. b. FALSE

Section 2.13

1. Duplicate data
2. a. TRUE
3. By placing common fields in tables that are related

Section 2.14

1. Get joined fields

2. A Subform is a form within a form.

3. When a user wants to display data from multiple tables where a one-to-many relationship occurs

Section 2.15

1. Segoe UI

2. b. FALSE

3. b. FALSE

4. The character dialog box

OpenOffice Volume III: Base Unit 3

Section 3.1

1. a. TRUE

2. A multi-level sort

3. a. TRUE

Section 3.2

1. Generic filters that can be used on any type of data, for each column of the table

2. a. TRUE

3. They display column-specific pull-down menus from which the user can set up a filter

4. To view a specific set of data within a larger database

Section 3.3

1. a. TRUE

2. Any data that was a match to one or more selected criteria would be displayed in the database

3. When trying to filter a table containing a large amount of data because by specifying the exact type of data necessary, it allows the user to quickly find the data without having to scroll through and identify the needed information manually.

4. On the Toolbar

Section 3.4

1. CTRL + X.

2. b. FALSE

3. Cut and Copy

4. CTRL + V

Section 3.5

1. The user can include all the columns from a particular table

2. a. TRUE

3. b. FALSE

4. Asking questions about the data

Section 3.6

1. It asks the user a series of questions, and then creates a query that fits the answers that were provided.

2. The Field Selection screen

3. The user has the ability to sort the query by any of the fields previously selected.

Section 3.7

1. F5

2. Performing a variety of mathematical functions

3. a. TRUE

Section 3.8

1. An integer that is 3 characters or less in length.

2. a. TRUE

3. An integer that is 19 characters or less in length.

4. Boolean data storage or True/False values

Section 3.9

1. 255 characters

2. a. TRUE

3. If numerical values are being entered into the table and a single number cannot exceed a certain amount.

Section 3.10

1. It's a section at the bottom of the page where the user is able to add page numbers

2. Through the Insert menu.

3. Allows the user to choose which fields will be used as part of the Report by selecting the desired fields from the Field List.

4. a. TRUE

Section 3.11

1. Three

2. Layout of data, Layouts of headers and footers, Orientation

3. b. FALSE

4. To determine the direction in which the Report is displayed.

Section 3.12

1. a. TRUE

2. The **Character** dialog box

3. a. TRUE

Section 3.13

1. a. TRUE

2. The user decides if the Combo Box value is saved into the table, or if the Combo Box value is only saved in the Form

3. The **Combo Box** combines the features of a textbox and a list box.

Section 3.14

1. b. FALSE

2. Edit Data button

3. a. TRUE

Section 3.15

1. The DELETE or BACKSPACE keys

2. b. FALSE

3. It unlocks the table.

www.ingramcontent.com/pod-product-compliance
Lightning Source LLC
Chambersburg PA
CBHW081237180526
45171CB00005B/446